179.9
Sm78
2015

THE DEAL

THE DEAL

*A Guide to Radical and
Complete Forgiveness*

RICHARD SMOLEY

JEREMY P. TARCHER/PENGUIN
a member of Penguin Group (USA)
New York

JEREMY P. TARCHER/PENGUIN
Published by the Penguin Group
Penguin Group (USA) LLC
375 Hudson Street
New York, New York 10014

USA · Canada · UK · Ireland · Australia
New Zealand · India · South Africa · China

penguin.com
A Penguin Random House Company

Most Tarcher/Penguin books are available at special quantity discounts for bulk purchase for sales
promotions, premiums, fund-raising, and educational needs. Special books or book excerpts also
can be created to fit specific needs. For details, write: Special.Markets@us.penguingroup.com.

Library of Congress Cataloging-in-Publication Data

Smoley, Richard.
The deal : a guide to radical and complete forgiveness / Richard Smoley.
p.   cm.
ISBN 978-0-399-17213-7
1. Forgiveness. I. Title.
BF637.F67S66   2015   2014027580
179'.9—dc23

Printed in the United States of America
1   3   5   7   9   10   8   6   4   2

Book design by Meighan Cavanaugh

For Aunt Martha

CONTENTS

THE PROBLEM

Let me begin with a confession. My sales skills are extremely limited. I've never mastered the art of the pitch or the close. My forays into the sales world have amounted to selling advertising for my college literary magazine (admittedly a hard task for anyone) and to a microcareer as a financial adviser, which mostly consisted of futile telemarketing.

So it's very much out of character for me to say what I am about to say. What I am offering you in this book is the best deal you have ever gotten in your life, or ever will. Even though I know nothing about you, I'm willing to make this claim with complete certainty. There are no products to buy, and there's nothing for you to spend money on. Very little time and effort are required, and you don't have to make any public statements or testimonies—because there is also nothing to sell. In fact, you never need tell anyone that you have even done it. All the same, it's the best deal that anyone will offer to you at any time in your life, past or present or future. For obvious reasons, I will simply call it the Deal.

The Deal is this: *You agree to give up all your grievances and resentments and grudges for good. In exchange, you ask for—and receive—complete forgiveness for yourself.*

Broken Glasses

Forgiveness is, we all agree, a great virtue, and we never seem to cease hearing its praises sung. But all is not quite what it seems with this business of forgiveness.

What, after all, do you think when you hear the words "I forgive you"? Maybe it sends a warm glow through you, but maybe it doesn't. You may remember times when someone said it condescendingly—as if they had the lordly power to bestow it as a favor on mere mortals like you. Possibly you can even remember times when you've said it that way yourself.

Then there is the breast-beating form of forgiveness—"I forgive you because we are all wretched scum. All have sinned. There is none righteous, no, not one." This hardly feels any better.

In fact, forgiveness seems to be best when it's the least ostentatious. If you look back on your life, you may find times when you have forgiven or been forgiven almost without noticing it at all. I'm reminded of a time when I was about ten. It was recess at school, and it was winter. Several of us were sliding on the ice. At one point I bumped into another kid by accident. He fell down, and the stem of his eyeglasses broke. I think I said I was sorry, but I really don't remember. One of the other kids said, "Wow! You're going to have to pay for those!" The kid whose glasses were broken didn't say anything.

I was very anxious for the rest of the day and night. I was sure that my parents would have to pay for the glasses, and, having no idea of how much they cost, I was terrified that the price would be stiff. Of course I said nothing. The next day I went to school dreading the consequences of my deeds. What greeted me was something I did not expect in the slightest. The kid with the broken glasses had a little bit of tape wrapped around the broken stem, and the glasses seemed to be holding together. He still didn't say anything, and I never worried about the problem again.

Was that forgiveness? It certainly wasn't forgiveness of any grandiose sort. It was simply a matter of letting the whole thing go. All the same, it was a tremendous relief to me, and I was grateful enough to remember the incident almost fifty years later.

From all of this, it seems clear that forgiveness can take more than one form. It can be, and often is, a simple matter of letting things drop. It need not involve blubbery reconciliations and lots of hugging. Of course those can happen too, and they can be intense and satisfying in their own way. But forgiveness is far richer and more wide-ranging than even the most intense emotional experience.

The Pleasures of Resentment

It seems that forgiveness in any form feels good. So if it feels good, why don't we do it more often?

Partly because it can also feel good *not* to forgive. There can be something delicious in holding a grievance, in mulling over someone else's wrongs and failings and viewing him through the lenses of condemnation. We could call this "the thrill of righteousness." In 1964, psychologist Eric Berne published a best seller called *Games People Play*. One of these games was called "Now I've Got You, You Son of a Bitch." As Berne put it, "This can be seen in classic form in poker games. White gets an unbeatable hand, such as four aces. At this point, if he is a NIGYSOB player, he is more interested in the fact that Black is at his complete mercy than he is in good poker or making money." Possibly the thrill of righteousness has something to do with this game.

Unfortunately, righteousness is the most dangerous of all weapons to wield. It's easily turned against the user. Say one of your fellow employees is regularly late for work. You find it delicious to contemplate this poor fool's tardiness and to congratulate yourself for your own punctuality. Then one day, for some reason or another, you are late for work yourself. The boss yells at you in front of everybody, including the coworker who you've been so comfortably despising. Suddenly all the fun has gone sour. The moral might be this: Beware the sin you condemn. It will be the next one that you commit.

Sometimes we also refuse to forgive because of our sense of justice. A recent study looked at how people differ from chimpanzees in their approach to fairness. Scientists tested this by means of the ultimatum game, which has two players: a proposer and a responder. They have to divide a quantity of goodies (which could be anything from cash to chocolates). The proposer chooses how much will go to him and how much to the responder. The responder has no choice but to take or leave the offer.

You might expect that the responder would accept any offer, no matter how small; after all, even a little is better than nothing.

That's what chimps do. But humans don't. Human responders will generally reject any offer smaller than around 20 percent—even if they don't get anything at all. They do this, it seems, to punish the proposer for his greed.

So, in a way, chimpanzees turn out to be more rational than humans. And yet researchers believe that this sense of fairness, and a willingness to punish someone who's being unfair even at a loss to oneself, is humanity's "killer app." It's what allows large social groups to form.

No doubt this sense of fairness has something to do with our reluctance to forgive. We want to punish someone who's gone beyond the bounds of fairness—but unfortunately we want to keep on punishing. At some point this "punishment" starts to go on and on in our own heads. We rehearse the wrong that we have suffered, we stew over it, we brood, and we sulk. And we do this even when the offender is nowhere in sight. Again the punishment is turned against the punisher.

Treacherous Armor

But possibly the most important reason that we hold on to grievances is that we believe they offer something to us. And what they offer, or appear to offer, is protection.

Think about it. To be free of grievances is to be innocent. And if you go around with your innocence exposed, you believe all the buzzards of life will suddenly swarm upon you to pick your bones white. Your grievances are like the hard face you wear when you're making your way through a bad neighborhood. They are your shield.

There is a grain of truth to this idea. All of us, as living beings, have a basic need to preserve ourselves. We react—sometimes violently—to anything that threatens our survival. Fear and anger are common types of this reaction. These responses are useful up to a point, but there is a problem: They continue long after the threat has passed. We often carry this fear and anger with us for a long time afterward—possibly years or decades—long after the emotions have outlived their value. These retained feelings can take the form of grievances and resentments. They do not help us survive. They are debilitating.

In fact, your grievances are your weak spot, the open wounds that anyone can prod to put you on the ground in an instant. Perhaps this is not readily apparent. To explain what I'm talking about, let's turn to politics.

I am not, by the way, putting forward any political agenda in this book. The Deal is open to people of any and all ideologies. But I do believe that people of any and all ideologies can be and are manipulated by their grievances.

Let's look at the political scene with some attempt at impartiality. No matter what ideology you believe in, you know what's really wrong with things. It's *them*. It's *their* fault. If it weren't for *them*, the world would be happy and safe and prosperous. But as it is, the world's problems seem to be beyond all hope of a solution. Why? Because *they* are always in the way, always on the alert to block anything good.

Whoever you are, I venture to guess that you have a *them*. So do I. Yours may or may not be the same as mine. It doesn't matter. The fault is all with *them*. In the United States as I write this in 2013, there are several large blocks of people who are united by their hatred of particular versions of *them*. This hatred is enormously useful, although not to the people who possess it. It's useful to any number of powerful interests who manipulate your hatred of *them*. These interests know how to set you snarling about *them*, and this knowledge—gained by enormous amounts of research in manipulating mass opinion—can be used to make you dance whatever jig they want you to.

With all this going on, it's no wonder that conspiracy theories abound, warning us of a secret cabal at the top who have us at their mercy. More likely, the truth is that there are any number of competing interests, each trying to set a particular group of people against a particular version of *them* and thereby gaining an advantage. Although no one of these interests is all-powerful, their strength, individually and collectively, is not to be denied. If you are susceptible (and all of us are to some extent), you can be made to love what these interests want you to love, hate whom they want you to hate, elect whom they want you to elect. You, like me, can easily be gotten to vote against your own best interests. This has been proved over and over.

I could go further into these issues of mass control and mass manipulation, but this doesn't serve my purpose here. I'm simply pointing out that, in the world of politics, your grievances are not protecting you. They are weakening and betraying you.

So it is in daily life. In the workplace, for example, you inevitably acquire allies and opponents—or, if you like, friends and enemies. In the complex world of alliances, one can easily turn

into the other. Someone you detest turns out to be very likable—
or very useful. Someone you thought was close to you turns into
an adversary.

Beyond a certain point, there is no avoiding this. It's what
makes human relations what they are. But it can be harmful to
you to hold on to a grudge when it serves your own best interests
to drop it. (Notice that I'm speaking purely in the language of
advantage and disadvantage; we will leave love, compassion, and
other higher things for later.) It's even worse to form a resentment
on a purely imaginary basis—for some slight or wrong that may
have been totally unintentional, or (which happens just as often)
is actually the doing of someone completely different. But the
human mind has a tendency to jump to conclusions. The ancient
Greeks associated the mind with the god Hermes. And Hermes
was a trickster. This was no accident.

Are You Your Team?

In any event, if you examine your mind with any amount of honesty, you will probably conclude that your grievances are doing
you no good whatsoever. Why, then, hang on to them?

I've already given a couple of reasons, but there is another, subtler, and more troubling one. Let me approach it by telling a story. This took place during my aforementioned microcareer as a financial adviser. One day we were all shepherded into a day-long seminar. It was one of those watered-down human potential workshops that seem to be popular in corporate America. They probably don't accomplish much, but they allow the company to congratulate itself for being "enlightened," and they give the employees a painless break from the routine.

As part of this particular workshop, we were asked to think of a symbol for ourselves. The leader of the seminar—who happened to be my boss—offered his own personal symbol. It was a half-full beer glass, which, I gathered, combined an innate optimism with a fondness for brewed beverages. It was, in its way, apt. My boss then went around the room and asked the forty or fifty participants to think of personal symbols for themselves. Most people were at an utter loss. About half could think of nothing more original than the logos of their favorite sports teams.

There's nothing wrong with being a sports fan (although I'm not one myself). But it is a little odd to be so deeply unaware of who you are that a team logo is the best symbol for yourself that you can come up with.

Of course, many fans genuinely identify with their teams. Eric Simons, author of *The Secret Lives of Sports Fans*, observes, "In the case of sports, there is compelling evidence that this is basically a real relationship in your brain. In a very real sense, the sports team becomes a part of you. You just feel like whatever success it achieves is a personal success, and whatever failure it has is a personal failure. You can't cut the team off without cutting off a part of yourself."

Up to a point this is all harmless enough. But for many people, being a fan is not only loving your own team—it's hating the other team. (Again you see *them* raising their heads.) Sometimes it looks as if hating the other team is the most enjoyable part.

So we have a curious little dynamic going on here. You don't know who you are. Maybe, in your own mind, you're your team. You are caught up in not only its triumphs and defeats, but in its grudges and grievances. In other words, *you have identified yourself with grievances*. You have *become* these grievances.

I've chosen sports fandom to introduce this idea partly because it's a light way to touch upon a disturbing fact about human nature. We nurture our grievances because we identify with them. We think we *are* our grievances. Of course, this happens much more easily and completely if you are unaware of the fact. (As soon as you become aware of it, you have introduced a distance, however slight, between yourself and the grievance. This, as we will see, is the gateway to freedom.)

Despite the occasional drunken brawl, sports fandom is a relatively mild form of this syndrome (at least in America, where things like soccer hooliganism are not especially popular). A fan may feel depressed for a day or so if his team has lost a big game, but this doesn't count for much in the scheme of things.

Identifying with grievances becomes much more dangerous when they belong to a race, nation, or religion. It becomes more dangerous still when these grievances have been ingrained by centuries of tradition. I don't want to single out any particular group of people, so I'll refrain from giving specific examples, but there are nations whose identities have crystallized around battles lost hundreds of years ago. This can be hard for Americans—with their notoriously short historical memory—to fathom, and in fact, it may be partly why Americans have trouble understanding much of the rest of the world.

In any event, you can see the problem: people identify with their religion and ethnicity. If these groups have a long memory of injustices perpetrated upon them—and if their identity has crystallized around these injustices—then a member of the group believes she has to take on these grievances as her own. Usually this is not a matter of conscious choice; it's ingrained from earliest childhood. If we can see this dynamic, suddenly a great deal of the conflict in the world today becomes much easier to understand. This feeling of collective grievance can lead to bitterness and hatred of the most vicious kind. As we know, there are people in the world today who are blowing themselves up for the sake of these grievances.

So far I've been speaking at a collective level, because the forces of identification are somewhat easier to see on this scale. But what I've said also holds true for individuals. There are people who have suffered injustice, harm, and crime in their lives, and these events have shaped their personal identities. To be sure, terrible things happen, and they have to be faced squarely and honestly: there is a balance between denial on the one hand and obsessively dwelling on past hurts on the other. But people harm themselves when they shape their self-images around victimhood. And it seems that those who have handled deep traumas the best have been those who have somehow managed to put the past behind them and gotten on with their lives. Is this forgiveness as, say, a minister would define it in a sermon? I don't know. From my own point of view, as I've said, forgiveness often seems to consist of letting offenses drop and moving on.

The Entertainment of Conscience

There's yet one more reason that people feel grievances. Again it has to do with self-image—but in a different way. People believe their grievances make them good people. They think their grievances are a protest against the evils of the world and that they would be bad people if they didn't hold them.

Let me explain. We all know that there are terrible injustices in the world—some so terrible that they are hard for the average middle-class American to imagine. Some (though relatively few) are brought to our attention through the media. "Someone should do something about this!" we think. Maybe someone will. But we ourselves are probably not going to do anything—and there are so many of these situations in the world that it's impossible for any one person to deal with them all. Deep down inside, we know this, and we feel guilty about it. We often deal with this guilt by turning it into outrage—which proves to ourselves, in some kind of roundabout way, that we are good and caring people and that we will not let these injustices pass unnoticed. Again, this outrage does no earthly good for anyone, but it does manage to soothe our discontent. Much of the media's coverage of wars and disasters seems to be designed to play into this dynamic. I call it "the entertainment of conscience." We are provided with news and images of horrors, we feel outraged, and thus we reassure ourselves of our own decency.

I'm not, by the way, trying to say that all forms of compassion are phony. The outrage that we feel is usually genuine enough. But often it is also futile. The spiritual teacher G. I. Gurdjieff spoke of this as the tendency "vainly-to-grow-sincerely-indignant" (to use his own odd punctuation) and he cited it as a sign of the waking sleep that dominates our lives.

Certainly it's easy to get caught up in this morass without even realizing what you are doing. During the Gulf War in 1991, I was talking to a friend of mine who said, "I'm really getting upset from all this war coverage." To which I replied, "Well, why don't you just stop watching it?" Her reply was honest: "I never thought of that."

The truth is that watching wars and disasters and crimes on TV will not make you a good person, no matter how much grief and compassion you may sincerely feel. Nor will these emotions make life the slightest bit better for those who are suffering. In fact, their suffering is often made worse by our need for this entertainment. When a woman has seen her child shot or her house float away, it can't be pleasant to have a reporter shove a microphone in her face and ask her to talk about her suffering for the amusement of the home audience.

"What, then, are we to do?" you may be asking. Just let it all go on? Yes, in a way. I *will* let it all go on, because there is nothing I can do about the vast majority of these situations, and my anger and outrage about them does no one the slightest bit of good— not even me. If I think that these emotions make me a good person, I am lying to myself. Good people help others; they do not go around feeling bad because they are doing nothing for others.

If I stopped here, it may well seem that I'm arguing for laziness and apathy. I'm not. I'm arguing against useless emotions. There *are* positive ways of acting in the world, things that you can do that are not futile, and I will get to these in due course.

Your Biggest Victim

Finally, there is the matter of forgiving yourself. You probably hold as many or more grievances against yourself than you do against the rest of the world combined. Usually we don't think in those terms, but, in fact, guilt and shame in most of their forms are nothing more than hostilities that we hold against ourselves. They can also take the form of regret—punishing yourself over and over for a bad decision you have made or think you have made.

I could go on for much longer, but the point is clear. The

grudges and resentments and hostilities that we go around with do us no good at all. We would be better off without them. To let go of these negative emotions is to forgive.

It's time to get to the Deal itself. To state it again, with the Deal *you agree to give up all your grievances and resentments and grudges for good. In exchange, you ask for—and receive—complete forgiveness for yourself.*

That is the Deal. You give up something that is harmful to you, and you get total forgiveness in its place. As I've said, no one will ever offer you anything better.

Well, then, let's get on with it.

2

DOING THE DEAL

Since people are so different, it's hard to predict how you personally will respond to the Deal. Of those who are attracted to it, some may plunge in and do it without further thought. Others may set this book aside—possibly for years—and then pick it up one day and do the Deal because it happens to be the right time for them. A good number will probably come to it in a time of extremity, when everything else has been tried and failed.

There is one reason to do it *now* rather than later—to spare yourself (and maybe others) needless suffering.

1. Set and Setting

As a general rule, I would recommend reading through this whole book before trying to do the exercise below. The later chapters will show you how to integrate the Deal into your daily life and will deal with questions and problems that may come up.

I want to stress, however, that the Deal itself consists only of the instructions in this chapter. If you follow them, you will have done the Deal. All the things that come after it are purely advisory.

The things you will need are very simple. You will need a half hour to an hour of uninterrupted time, with no distractions, electronic or otherwise, and you will need a place where you will not be disturbed. You can go to a pleasant and secluded spot outdoors, or you can use your bedroom or even your office if you can be sure no one will bother you for that long. There should be as little noise as possible, and the temperature should be comfortable enough that you are not aware of it one way or another. It may also be useful to have something to write with.

You can make this exercise far more elaborate if you like. You can set up a room—such as a meditation room, which some people have—with candles and incense and photographs of a number of the most important people in your life who you want to forgive. There are those who are inclined toward ritual, and they may find this kind of preparation helpful, particularly if it's done with awareness and a recollection of the ultimate purpose of the exercise. They can also use prayers and meditations and readings from inspirational texts that will help put them in the right frame of mind. But none of this is necessary, and it is best avoided if you think you will become so preoccupied with the details that they will bury the central purpose. The Deal can be done in any setting in which you find yourself free from disturbance. You can even do it while riding in a plane if you are comfortable with that: for many people, this is the only time they really have to themselves.

Probably the most practical way to do the following exercise is to have this book in hand, read a paragraph or two, follow the directions, and then continue. You can also read the directions aloud, record your own voice, and play it to yourself while you actually do the practice. If several people decide to do this exercise together, one of them can be chosen to serve as the reader. The reader should read the directions slowly and attentively, pausing at appropriate moments. The reader can do the exercise along with everyone else; she may have done it herself first, or she can do it later on her own, perhaps with somebody else reading.

2. Centering

It's best to sit upright in a comfortable chair. You can conceivably do this lying down, but you are very likely to fall asleep if you do, and you should avoid that. Your position should be relaxed but alert. You don't need to sit in any elaborate cross-legged positions unless you're perfectly at ease with them. This is not a yoga exercise, and from the point of view of the Deal, one posture has no more merit than another.

Begin by closing your eyes and sensing your body in your seat. You may be aware of your back against the chair, your feet on the floor, your hands on your thighs or wherever they happen to be. See if you can consciously sense them from the inside. If the mind settles, you can feel the sensations rise and fall, in different parts of the body at different moments. You may feel them as waves or ripples of energy.

Now let your attention come to the breath. You may take a couple of deep breaths to relax, but otherwise don't try to control or manipulate the flow. Just let it go in and out and watch its progress as if you were sitting by a pleasant brook and watching the water go by. Continue for a couple of minutes.

While you have been doing this, thoughts and images and

pictures have no doubt been arising in your mind, whether you
want them to or not. It's hard to stop this stream of consciousness
(as it's sometimes called), and for the purposes here, it is not
necessary. Simply sit back and watch the images come up in your
mind's eye as if you were watching a film. Their content does not
matter one way or another. What is important is that you watch
these things in your mind clearly and impartially, almost as if
they belonged to somebody else. Usually you think these thoughts
and images *are* you. But if you can step back and watch them from
a distance, you must be something other than these things.

Emotions—anxiety, anger, or for that matter cheer or joy—
may come up along with the thoughts and images; an image may
trigger an emotion, or emotions that you feel may bring up images
in the mind. Thoughts and emotions are tightly connected, so
simply watch them all together as they arise in their turn.

At this point your mind may have settled down and calmed
itself to some degree. Let your attention return to your breath
while focusing on the area in the center of your chest near your
heart. See if you can make some kind of connection between the
breath and this area of the chest. You may feel a warmth in your
chest, a tightness, or some other sensation. Simply allow your attention to rest there for a few seconds.

3. Release from the Present

Now go to a secret place in your heart. Don't think about it or ask what it means—just do it. You will probably feel that you are in a very quiet, still, and secluded space where no one can find you. This, in fact, is the truth.

Now, as you rest in this secret place in the heart, look in your mind's eye at things you think you've done wrong in the recent past—something you said today that you shouldn't have, commitments you haven't kept, debts you haven't paid. Think also of all the things that are currently bothering you. You may, for example, feel that you don't have enough money or are lacking a lover or dislike the place you're living in. Possibly you feel these problems are your fault.

Let your attention then go to what you think of as your personal failings. You may think "I'm too lazy," "I'm too shy," "I eat too much," and make other such judgments. Images associated with these things may arise; so may emotions of one kind or another.

Again let your attention go to the sensations of the body. How does your body feel when you have these things on your mind? Does it feel light or heavy? Is there tension or tightness or pain anywhere?

Now, here in this secret place in your heart, ask yourself, *"Do I want to be released from all these things?"*

Notice that you are not asking *how* this will happen. You are simply asking yourself in full sincerity whether you want to be freed from these burdens.

What is your answer? If it is *no*, ask yourself if this is because you somehow think it is impossible to be released in this way. But you are not concerned right now with what is possible. You are merely deciding what you want. If your answer is still *no*, then bring this exercise to a close by returning your attention to the sensations of the body and allowing your eyes to open in their own time.

(By the way, there is nothing wrong in deciding not to go further with this process. It may simply mean that it is not for you, or that it's not for you at this time. You are free to try it again later on, at any point. This is not a limited-time offer.)

If the answer to the above question is *yes*, take a deep breath and release all of these oppressive thoughts and images.

4. Release from the Past

Now let your mind go back further in time. You may think of the recent past, say the last year or so. Think of the things you feel guilty for—saying something cruel to someone, breaking a promise, cheating on a lover. You may feel this guilt even for very small things—missing an appointment, failing to return a phone call. You may notice that you are feeling bad about many things that didn't actually hurt anyone else; they may be very minor, or they may involve ways in which you have hurt yourself—failing to stand up for yourself, making what you think of as stupid mistakes. You didn't fight back against the school-yard bully, you were too timid to ask the beautiful girl in your class out for a date, and so on.

Ask again, "Do I want to be released from all these things?"

Now go back in your mind's eye through the years, almost as if you are watching a film being played backward.

You may think of things that you've failed to do in your life: lovers you've cheated on, lies you've told, people you've hurt, school courses that you didn't finish. Allow these offenses to surface almost at random. Again, you may well see a mixture of actual occasions when you did some harm and others where you feel vaguely guilty, even though no one was hurt or even noticed what you did.

Take as much time as you want to look at these things. Again, emotions may come up; let them. You may discover little corners of pain and regret that you didn't know existed.

Follow this train of thought as far back in your memory as you can—to your earliest memories, and perhaps beyond. Ask yourself, "Did I do anything wrong in a past life?" Even if you don't believe in reincarnation, you may find it useful to ask this question, because some surprising things may come up.

Of course there's no way you can think of all the things you've done that you feel bad about—that isn't possible. Only make sure you are not deliberately excluding anything. (It's possible that you may be excluding something unconsciously. If this is happening, you may feel a sense of discomfort or irritation. In this case, allow yourself to feel any physical sensations connected with this discomfort. As you do, some images or ideas or emotions may come to mind, giving you a sense of what you're excluding. Once you're aware of what it is, simply include it in the things you want to be released from.)

Now ask yourself a third time, "Do I want to be released from all these things?"

You may hear something deep inside you and say yes, or you

may feel a sense of comfort, lightness, or warmth. Take a deep breath and let it out.

At this point you can open your eyes for a moment or two if you like, or even get up and stretch and walk around the room or whatever space you're in for a minute or so. Don't break the space, however; stay in the room or remain near your seat if you are outside.

5. Releasing Others

Now take your seat again. Let your eyes close, and let your attention return to your breath and the sensations of your body.

Bring to your mind someone with whom you are angry or irritated or against whom you are holding a grudge. Anyone you dislike is certainly a candidate.

Chances are someone will come readily to mind. Picture this person as if he or she is standing before you. Notice the expression on this person's face.

Ask yourself now, *"Am I willing to forgive this person?"*

If the answer is *no*, just remember that you want to be released from many things yourself, and this is an essential part of the process. Ask yourself again, *"Am I willing to forgive this person?"*

If the answer is still *no*, then you can bring the exercise to a close, open your eyes, and go about your business.

If the answer is *yes*, let your image of the person fade in your mind.

Now let your attention go to all the grievances, grudges, and hostilities you are holding. This includes anyone and anything you are angry with, to whatever degree. Examples include co-workers you don't get along with, a spouse or ex-spouse who has hurt you, neighbors, family members, friends, and of course enemies. Make sure to include larger entities (such as governments, organizations, political parties, and churches) as well as figures you don't know personally—political and religious leaders, even celebrities and sports figures. Focus on those who are present in your mind right now—the ones who are irritating you the most in your daily life.

And, of course, be sure to include yourself. The grievances we hold against ourselves are often the most intense and deeply rooted, covering not only cases where we have done genuine harm but those in which we feel regret for minor errors, slips of the tongue, lapses in etiquette, and so forth. People frequently go through excruciating anguish over very small things.

Now ask yourself, *"Am I willing to forgive all of these people?"*

If the answer is *no*, ask yourself which person or persons you don't want to forgive. Remind yourself that your grievances do not harm this person in any way; you are the only one they hurt. Then ask yourself again, *"Am I willing to forgive this person?"*

If the answer is still *no*, then you can bring the exercise to a close, open your eyes, and go about your business.

If the answer is *yes*, let the images of these people fade in your mind.

Finally, let your attention go to your past, including all the people that you can think of who have ever hurt you. Again, you don't need to think of every last person. But let as many individuals as possible come to your mind, and make sure not to consciously exclude anyone. People you think of may include your family, teachers, schoolmates, relatives, friends, past lovers, and acquaintances. (Again, be sure to include yourself.) You may even let your mind go back to lives that you suspect you have lived before this one, and see what images arise.

Let your mind now go to the evils of the world—the sorrows, sufferings, atrocities, torture, killing, environmental damage, cruelty, and privation. Do not, in this exercise, try to look for or think of an answer. You are not trying to explain or understand the evils of the world.

Feelings and emotions may come up, including anger, hatred, resentment, and fear. If they do, again note them attentively but dispassionately, as if they belonged to someone else, and then let them go.

Ask, *"Am I willing to forgive all these people and all these things?"*

If the answer is *no*, focus on the person or people against whom you still hold a grudge. Remember again that no matter how much this person may have hurt you, your anger does no harm to him or her; it hurts only you.

Ask again, *"Am I willing to forgive all these people?"*

If the answer is still *no*, then you can bring the exercise to a close, open your eyes, and go about your business.

6. Finalizing the Deal

If the answer is *yes*, let the images fade from your mind for the time being. Then focus again on your body and your breath. Let your attention return to all the things you want to be forgiven for. You can picture the images and emotions associated with these as being located in front of you to one side—say the left.

As you look at all these things, say to yourself, *"I ask to be forgiven for all these things."* If it's appropriate in your case, you can ask God or Jesus or Spirit to forgive you.

Let your attention now focus on all the people and persons you want to forgive. You can picture them also as being located in front of you to one side—say the right.

Say to yourself, *"I forgive all of you for everything."* You can also add, *"I ask God [or Jesus or Spirit] to forgive you for everything as well."*

Now release all the images, thoughts, feelings, and people that you see in front of you. You may, for example, picture them as dissolving in white light, or standing in enormous balloons that you release and let float away. Allow yourself to feel free of all these burdens.

Say to yourself now, *"It is done. I have forgiven everything and I accept forgiveness for everything."*

This is the Deal: You forgive everything and are forgiven for everything. It is the law, and it works: *Your debts are forgiven as you have forgiven your debtors.*

7. Taking Action

There is one last step. Ask yourself if there is anything you need to do as a result of this process. Are there people you need to speak to, to say you forgive or ask forgiveness of? Do you need to make amends to anyone? This is entirely a matter of your own individual initiative. Please note this important point: *You are not required to take any specific external action as a result of the Deal.* You do not have to tell anyone about it or do anything at all. *Any action you take is purely a matter of your own choice and volition.* I will explain why later.

Nevertheless, chances are that you will decide to do some specific things as a result of this process. Chances are also that you will know almost instantaneously what these things are. If there are more than one or two, or if you think you will forget, you might want to write them down.

Take a few deep breaths and relax before opening your eyes. See how you feel now as compared to the way you did when you started this exercise. If any powerful emotions have come up, allow yourself to feel them without any self-criticism or repression.

When you are ready, return to your ordinary state of consciousness, and stand up.

8. Integration

If a bathroom or sink is available (or if you are near a source of water outdoors), it would be helpful to go and wash your hands and face with the conscious intention of cleansing yourself of all the grievances and resentments from the past. If this is not possible right away, try to remember to do it as soon as possible later. This action is not absolutely necessary, but it will help anchor this process in you, because there is a part of your mind that responds best to physical stimuli.

The Deal is a major achievement, and it is one that very few people have accomplished. Make sure that you acknowledge this, and honor yourself accordingly. However you may have seen yourself in the past, you can now recognize that you are a holy being, with the power to give and receive blessings to an infinite degree. Your actions today will have consequences far beyond those you may have expected, and they will benefit and heal, not only yourself and the people you have thought of, but many others you do not know and may never even meet.

To repeat: If you have followed these instructions, you have done the Deal. All the other instructions in this book are merely advisory.

It can be useful to take some time—a few hours, if possible—to be by yourself and reflect on what you have just done. You can take a walk in a pleasant setting, you can sit and have a quiet cup of coffee in a café, or you can lie on the sofa and daydream for a while. While your responses may be subtle and may take some time to make themselves felt, they can also be thrilling (and liberation from your grievances can be very thrilling). In any case, it's generally best to digest these feelings on your own rather than telling everyone (or anyone) right away. There will be time for all that later.

In fact, it's generally a good idea to be careful about whom you discuss the Deal with. Although forgiveness is widely praised, many people think of it as rather naive and childish—certainly in any kind of comprehensive form. So even your family and friends might be inclined to dismiss or deride the step you have taken. Particularly for the first few days, I would recommend talking about the Deal only with people who you are sure will be sympathetic to and supportive of it. They may not include your spouse; in fact, husbands and wives can be extremely dismissive of each other's efforts to free themselves from negativity. It is partly why you are not required to tell anyone about the Deal. This is a profound step to take, and it's a good idea to protect it, particularly while it is still young and vulnerable within you.

Another word of caution: You may feel a tremendous sense of euphoria and exhilaration as a result of the Deal. Thus you could suddenly decide to take some radical steps in your life. *It would be wise to avoid doing anything of this kind for a minimum of three days after doing the Deal.* What is and isn't a radical step is, of course, a matter of judgment. It certainly isn't a radical step to smile at a coworker whom you used to hate. But if you have an overwhelming urge to give all your money to charity, quit your job to work with the poor in India, or reconnect with your alcoholic and abusive ex-husband, it would be a good idea to wait for at least three days, and probably longer, before making such a move.

9. Reinforcement

Finally, you may want to reinforce what you have done with a daily spiritual practice of some sort. I have made every effort to avoid time-consuming projects, since very few people have extra time, but it can be useful to meditate daily. There are innumerable forms of meditation, and while many are extremely easy to describe (concentrating on the breath, for example), it's best to be introduced to the practice by a qualified teacher with whom you can discuss your progress and difficulties. The particular type of meditation you choose will depend mostly on personal taste and predilection as well as on your spiritual affinities.

At some point during your daily meditation, you can remember the Deal by saying to yourself: "I have forgiven the world," or "I forgive everyone and everything," and "I accept total forgiveness for myself," or "I forgive myself totally." Again, the specific choice of words is not crucial. The important point is to remember that you have forgiven and have received forgiveness in turn. You may want to put these statements in the form of a prayer to God or Spirit if that's appropriate to your beliefs.

Even if you don't meditate, it's beneficial to remind yourself of the Deal at least once a day by making statements of the kind suggested above. You can do this while drinking a cup of coffee, driving your car to work, or after going to bed at night, just before you go to sleep.

Another useful practice is simply to send a thought of total love, peace, and blessing to everyone in the world. You can do this silently at any and all times of day. You may also want to mentally send blessings to people who are around you at home, at work, or at public places.

You will not necessarily see any external results from doing this—but on occasions you might be surprised by what happens.

3

WHY IT WORKS

At this point you may be asking how this man, the author of this book, whoever he is, can hold out the promise of total forgiveness to you. Do I have the power to forgive sins? No more than you, and no less.

In that case, where does the power to forgive come from?

The Law and the Loophole

Let's begin by looking at this issue from the point of view of karma. The word *karma* comes from Sanskrit, the sacred language of India, but it has made its way into mass culture. (My children were watching a cartoon recently in which it was used by a bunch of hippies.) Originally it simply meant "doing" or "action," but its usual meaning has to do with the law of cause and effect. Sometimes karma is even defined as the law of cause and effect, but this is not totally accurate. Karma means not only that certain causes have certain effects—which is obvious enough—but that a cause produces an effect *like itself.* That is, a good deed produces good and a bad deed produces evil. Furthermore, the effects of this deed come back sooner or later to the doer.

The idea of karma is most often found in Hinduism and Buddhism, as well as in New Age contexts, where the influence of Eastern spirituality is strong. Thus it may sound a little foreign to people schooled in the Judeo-Christian tradition. But the same concept is found there, in the Bible, for example: "For they have sown the wind, and they shall reap the whirlwind" (Hosea 8:7), or "Whatsoever a man soweth, that shall he also reap" (Galatians 6:7; biblical quotations in this book are taken from the Authorized King James Version unless otherwise noted). This is nothing more than the teaching of karma put in slightly different language.

If all of this is sounding a bit too religious for you, here is the same idea, expressed in Ralph Waldo Emerson's essay "Compensation": "Punishment is a fruit that unsuspected ripens within the flower of the pleasure which concealed it. Cause and effect, means and ends, seed and fruit, cannot be severed; for the effect already blooms in the cause, the end preexists in the means, the fruit in the seed." In fact, Emerson's whole essay is really about karma, although he doesn't use the term. (He does mention *nemesis*, which is the ancient Greek word for retribution.)

You can call it karma or compensation or nemesis, but the idea is a universal one, and, I would say, deep down inside we know the truth of it. It's sometimes true, of course, that the wicked prosper and the righteous suffer. Why this should be so is a larger question than I want to discuss here, but it also seems true that most people most of the time get exactly what they should get. As the proverb says, "When you're twenty, you have the face you were born with; when you're fifty, you have the face you deserve."

In one sense the idea of karma is comforting. The human soul hungers for justice, and perhaps we have this need because such a thing genuinely exists in the universe. (Would we ever be thirsty if there were no such thing as water?) But in another sense the idea of karma is disturbing, even monstrous. You have done something wrong; the repercussions of your deeds are bound to come back to you; that is the law and it is implacable. And all of us have done something wrong at some point or another. As Hamlet said, "Use every man after his desert, and who should 'scape whipping?" There is no way out of the law of karma.

Except one.

It is forgiveness.

Debt Management

The law of karma is inexorable: it is a law like the laws of physics and there is no avoiding it. But if karma means that you will get as you have given, forgiveness is the answer. If you forgive, by the law of karma, you yourself are entitled to forgiveness. While there isn't a lot of emphasis on forgiveness in Buddhism, we see this point spelled out, clearly and obviously, in the Lord's Prayer: "Forgive us our debts as we have forgiven our debtors."

For Christians, who know this prayer by heart, my wording of this line may sound peculiar. Isn't it "trespasses" rather than "debts"? And isn't it "as we forgive" rather than "as we have forgiven"?

No, actually, it isn't. What I have given you above is a literal translation from the Greek of the Gospel of Matthew (the New Testament was originally written in Greek). While some people make a great fuss about the literal truth of the Bible, it's also true that sometimes people don't take the Bible literally enough. The actual word for "debts" is *opheilēmata*—which comes from a root meaning "to owe." The word is also used to refer to a workman's wages.

Many commentators tend to gloss over this difference and assume that this word really has to do with sins. I think they're mistaken. Actually, there is a great deal in the parables of Christ about forgiving monetary debts, and I suspect that this is no accident. It's partly because a great deal of what we need to forgive—and to be forgiven for—aren't sins in any genuine sense of the word. They are little obligations—social duties, large and small—that we may have failed to fulfill. Monetary debts serve as a symbol for these obligations. Even if they are not sins or crimes, we know we have come up short and we feel guilty about them. We even reflect this view in the way we talk: "I *owe* him a call"; "I *owe* her a birthday card." If you fail to call someone or send a birthday card, this is not a sin in anyone's book. But these failings weigh on us all the same—sometimes more than genuine offenses, which we tend to put out of our minds whenever we can. Some people may feel guilty about failing to return one person's phone call while forgetting that they have ruined another person's life.

Forgiveness is not complete unless we take all these things into account—the petty obligations, the Christmas presents we didn't give, the dinner invitations we didn't return, as well as the offenses and sins and crimes.

And yes, as a matter of fact, it is "as we have forgiven our debtors." (Technically the verb form used here is an aorist, a certain kind of past tense in ancient Greek.) This detail is important too. The usual form—"forgive us our debts as we forgive our debtors"—implies something a bit different. When I think of it, I have the image of a pair of thugs cautiously exchanging hostages. But the correct translation makes it our job to do the forgiving first.

There is no escape from guilt or grievance or even fear for the future except for forgiveness. Peace of mind is unthinkable without it. Unless you forgive, you live in a forest of enemies, and you never know when they will strike. But when you forgive, those anxieties vanish, to be replaced by tranquility. Perhaps not immediately, but soon, and as forgiveness takes root and grudges and resentments begin to wither away, life starts to offer vistas you could not have imagined before. The enormous part of your mind that was taken up with slights and offenses is now available for genuine creativity.

Does God Alone Forgive?

Recently in a magazine I saw a listing for a film called *Only God Forgives*. Certainly this title reflects a widespread belief.

In that case, we may find ourselves asking exactly who or what God is. In the old days, people imagined God as a gray-bearded man in the sky who had made human beings as a child fashions dolls out of clay. (Some of the ancient myths actually put it this way.) Today we have refined our conceptions somewhat, and the picture of the old man in the sky has fallen into disfavor.

Recently my sons, who are four and five, asked me out of the blue what God is. The answer that came to my mind was "God is where everything comes from. God is the Source of everything." It was a good enough answer to satisfy them, at least for the time being, and since then I haven't come up with a better one. Is God ultimately personal (as Christianity claims) or impersonal (as some Eastern religions say)? My own answer is this: If God is the Source of everything, then God must be larger or greater than any person we can imagine. At the same time, *we* are persons, and God possesses infinite capacities, so God—whatever he or she or it or they may be in an ultimate sense—can respond to us personally.

As for forgiveness, we as humans can forgive sins or "debts" that are owed to us personally. But it seems to be true that we can only receive total forgiveness from a higher level of consciousness and being than we are used to in daily life. We often identify this higher level with God.

All of us have our own images of God, and while these are useful in helping us to conceive of something that is beyond our understanding, they are all limited as well. We may forget this and start to think that these images are ultimately real or complete. This used to be called idolatry. In the past, people were much more oriented toward what they could see and touch, so they made physical images of their gods and forgot that they were only images. Today we are more clever: we know that statues and paintings are not to be identified with God, but instead we identify God with concepts and mental images. Sometimes these can be extremely complex and elaborate, but in any event we will necessarily conceive of God using concepts and images, because that is how our minds work. At the same time we need to remember that such a view is ultimately limited and inaccurate. As long as we remember this fact and remain humble about the ideas of God that we hold, they can be useful.

More and more people today think of God in impersonal terms, as a kind of force or energy or consciousness that pervades the universe. From the point of view of the Deal, this does not matter. It's true that the Deal involves asking for forgiveness from God or a higher power, however you understand that power, but it does not insist upon any particular view of God. Others might even deny the existence of a higher force or power entirely. In this case, they might ask forgiveness from the highest and best parts of themselves, however those are understood. You are not being asked to accept any particular religion or theology with the Deal; you have your own understanding, and that is good enough. You are merely asked to forgive and be forgiven.

How can we be so sure that God will forgive all our sins? For those who see things through the perspective of karma, it's inevitable. It will be done to us as we have done to others—there is no changing that. But others may have some serious doubts about whether God's forgiveness comes so easily.

I myself have done forgiveness work (imperfectly, I admit) for more than thirty years now, and I'm willing to say this much: If you feel that God cannot or will not forgive you, it's virtually certain that one of two things is going on. In the first place, you may think that certain things you have done are beyond the pale of forgiveness. In that case, you may want to identify those things (and you may not always be conscious of them), look at them, and ask forgiveness for them anyway.

In the second place, there may be something that you may not want to forgive in someone else. Again, you may not even be conscious of this. But if you want to do the Deal and enjoy the peace of mind that complete forgiveness offers, you'll need to dig this out of the recesses of your mind and offer it up as well.

The Partial Deal

Some may wonder if it's possible to do a partial Deal—to just forgive some things and ask in turn that some things be forgiven for us. Of course a little forgiveness is better than none, but this attempt at partial deliverance is likely to cause problems. How do you decide whom and what to forgive? As I've said, we tend to view our sins and debts in terms of transactions. Exactly how do you reckon the trade-off? Someone borrowed twenty dollars and has never paid you back. Another has borrowed five hundred. Do you forgive only the one who owes you twenty? Or neither? Or both? How do you draw the line? For another example, say your husband has had two affairs, while you have had only one. Does that mean that you forgive him for one of the two affairs and still stay angry with him on account of the other?

All this may sound peculiar, but the human mind tends to think this way. As soon as you make forgiveness a partial and discretionary matter, the calculus of emotional computations comes into play. You justify some offenses while still condemning others. Soon all the grudges and resentments come tumbling back in, and you are back where you started. You will save yourself a lot of mental and emotional confusion if you are willing to do the Deal wholesale.

4

LIVING THE DEAL

Assuming that you have followed the instructions for the Deal to the best of your ability, what next? What sort of life does the Deal commit you to? The instructions for this process are very simple, straightforward, and self-contained. You have forgiven the world, and you have accepted forgiveness. That is enough. Any action you take as a result will be entirely your own choice.

In biblical times, the Israelites were supposed to celebrate a jubilee every seven years (with a more comprehensive one every forty-nine years). Slaves (at least Hebrew slaves) were to be freed, and mortgaged land was to be returned. Whether this practice was actually ever carried out is open to question, but at any rate this was the idea.

The jubilee wiped out debts; it did not prevent them from accumulating again. People fell into slavery (often as a result of financial debt), land was mortgaged, and so on. That was why the jubilee had to be repeated in a seven-year cycle.

You can think of the Deal as a kind of jubilee in this sense. All sins are forgiven, all offenses wiped away. What then? Is it realistic to imagine that life will turn into a paradise, in which you neither do nor experience anything that requires forgiving?

This is probably not going to happen. So, then, having done the Deal, are you required to practice total forgiveness for the rest of your life?

As a matter of fact, if you go back and read the instructions, you will see that they say nothing of the kind. You have agreed to wipe away past grievances, and you have asked that grievances against you be taken away as well. No mention was made of what you might or might not do in the future.

This was no accident. To make an act of complete forgiveness is not a small gesture. You have let go of a tremendous number of things with which you identified and which you held close to yourself in the mistaken belief that they were valuable to you. This is difficult enough, and it would be unfair to ask any more of you at the outset. So you were not asked to make any promises about the future.

Nor were you asked to repeat the Deal. This is why: Many of us are critical and perfectionistic about ourselves. We often have an underlying sense that we are doing things wrong, that nothing we do is ever quite right or satisfactory. From the point of view of the Deal, this attitude too needs to be forgiven and released. Thus no specific provisions were made for repeating the Deal. Doing it once and for all can be enough.

All the same, you may feel that there is unfinished business, that things have come up that you didn't deal with completely the first time. Thus, of course, you can repeat the Deal as often as you feel it is necessary—even daily if need be. If, however, you reach the point where the process starts to feel mechanical or perfunctory, then you have probably done as much as you can for now, and it would be wise to stop, at least for the time being.

Reneging

You can even renege on the Deal. That choice is certainly open to you. You are free at any point to decide that it was utter nonsense and that you are going back to the way things were. I strongly doubt that as a result you will be struck down by the finger of the Almighty or will be carried off to the flames of perdition by hordes of gibbering demons. I would, in fact, imagine that nothing particular would happen at all. Except for one thing.

You will get what you asked for. If you choose to go back to life as you knew it before, your wish will be granted. You can have all your guilt, your hatreds, your resentments, and your hostilities returned to you immediately at no cost. But there is a barb to this, and it's only fair to warn you about it. *You may not feel as comfortable with your grievances as you did in the past.* In fact, you may find them much more irritating.

Why? If you do the Deal sincerely and thoroughly, you will, I believe, enjoy at least a taste of spiritual and psychological freedom. You will have a sense, however fleeting, of what life can be like without the burdens that practically everyone takes for granted. It will not be pleasant to take them up again.

Say a man is kept in solitary confinement in a windowless cell for thirty years. He gets used to his imprisonment; he has no other choice. His cell becomes familiar and maybe comfortable, and he starts to think of it as home—as, in fact, it is.

One day this man is taken outside and brought to a park on a sunny day with perfect weather. He walks around for an hour or two, and he becomes used to seeing sunlight and sky and trees again. Then he is taken back to his cell.

This little respite, no matter how welcome, will not necessarily make his life better. It may remind him of how cramped and confined and stinking his cell is, and he may find his imprisonment far more unbearable than before. This is what it can be like to renege on the Deal.

Relapse and Recovery

Of course, very few people are likely to actively and consciously make such a repudiation. Who deliberately turns her back on forgiveness? One would be reluctant to do this, if only for the sake of one's self-image as a good person. Far more likely is the possibility that you will let the Deal fade from your life.

The Deal is not a twelve-step or a recovery program (as a matter of fact, I have no direct experience with these). Nevertheless, it is *like* a recovery program in one sense: it attempts to cure you of your addiction to resentments. In some ways this is harder than curing yourself of a drug or alcohol habit. Society looks down upon alcoholics and drug addicts. They are despised and sometimes persecuted. If they try to clean up, they are given a certain amount of praise, and if they succeed, they are congratulated.

The same cannot be said of the addiction to grievances. There is little or no social support for this kind of recovery. Society regards grudges and resentments as good and right and just—or, at the very least, as a fundamental part of the way things are. The idea that you might be able to give these things up rarely occurs to anybody, and when it does, it's often dismissed as naive.

As a result, you will have to be a bit cagey about the way you incorporate the Deal into your life. Take the matter of discussing it with people you know. Rather than going into a long discourse, you might simply say, "I'm trying to be more forgiving" or "I'm trying to bring more forgiveness into my life." This makes it easier for the other person to accept, because total forgiveness can sound too idealistic and harebrained if taken out of context. People may well reply by arguing that there are certain things that shouldn't be forgiven, by asking how you could forgive [insert your favorite monster of history here], and so on. Simply saying you want to be more forgiving—which everyone approves of, at least in theory— is much less challenging and is much less likely to arouse opposition. If you sense that the person is more receptive and if it feels appropriate to you, then you can start to talk about the Deal.

Let's assume in any case that you would like to bring more forgiveness into your life. As I've said, this is a type of recovery, although unlike the better-known forms, there is no immediate pain upon withdrawal. Letting go of grievances feels good right away, and there is no discomfort that attends upon it. The only thing you may feel is a certain kind of void within yourself. Because so much of your mind has been taken up with resentments, you may literally find yourself wondering what you should think about now that you don't have them anymore. The answer is, of course, to start thinking about things that you find interesting and pleasurable.

Admittedly, there is a strong habit of mind that inclines us toward resentment. It is very likely to reassert itself fairly soon after you do the Deal—certainly within a few days at the very latest. For most people, this is not something that you banish with a snap of the fingers. Some retraining of the thoughts and emotions is needed.

The Little Things

Let's start with the simplest and easiest problems: passing day-to-day irritations. Someone cuts you off on the highway; the person ahead of you in the supermarket checkout line is dawdling; a clerk gives you a sour look while handing you your receipt. These have no great meaning in themselves; they usually involve strangers you will never see again. All the same, an experience like this can set you off on a hostile train of thought. It may lead you to brood upon all the other slights and humiliations you have to endure in life (completely innocently, of course, since you never do anything like this to anyone else). Or, especially if it happens in the morning, you may think of it as a kind of omen—telling yourself, "This is going to be one of those days" and waiting for the next person who comes along to aggravate you.

In these situations, the first thing to do is notice what is going on. This is not as easy as it sounds, since much of our mental chatter is automatic and goes on almost without our conscious consent. Years ago I had a friend who had to teach her dog to stop barking. "The first thing you do," she told me, "is teach the dog that it's barking." If the dog isn't aware of what it's doing, it won't know how to stop.

The same is true with the human mind. If you are starting to brood and sulk, the first thing to do is notice that this is going on. Obviously it's best if you can spot your reaction immediately, but it's common for people to find themselves in negative moods for minutes or hours or even days while barely being aware of what's going on or of what started it.

So first notice that you are indulging in negative emotion. In some cases this very act can stop the whole process, because it may derail the train of thought that was headed in this direction. At other times stronger medicine may be needed.

The easiest and simplest thing to do, in my experience, is to let the emotion drop. As I said in chapter 1, I believe forgiveness often has much more to do with simple letting go than with histrionic reconciliations. A man cut you off on the highway; it irritates you, but no harm is done. Simply let it go and let your mind move on to something more agreeable. You will not benefit in the slightest from a long internal diatribe about the increasing rudeness of drivers on the road or the manners of "those people" (if the driver belongs to a particular group that you dislike). You will benefit even less from recollecting everything you have heard or seen about road rage, of people killing one another over little things like this, or wherever your thoughts happen to take you. These thoughts are useless and harmful, and you can simply let them go.

How? you may ask. It's curious: if someone told you to drop a hammer, it would never for a second occur to you to ask *how*. You know how to let things drop, and you have done it since you were a baby. Letting an emotion drop is a bit harder, but only because we haven't been taught how.

Try this experiment: Think of things that make you feel angry and let your emotions rise up against them. You feel a sense of outrage, indignation, furor. Your body starts to tense, and you put a hard and determined look on your face. You are angry!

Now simply let the anger drop—all of it, the thoughts that you were dwelling on, the tightness in your muscles, the heat in your veins. Simply let it go. Your state of mind returns to normal. You were angry for a few seconds, and you let it go.

Now feel happy. Think of things that you find joyful and exciting. Smile, or even laugh—just because you have decided to. Let your heart and mind soar with joy and exaltation.

Let the happiness drop. Simply let it all go and return to your ordinary state of consciousness. You are now neither happy nor angry; your feelings are completely neutral.

An exercise like this points out one fact: our emotions are, at least to some extent, within our control. I doubt that we can consciously change long-term dispositions of feeling or character in the same way, unless a powerful shock of some kind sends them in the opposite direction. But it *is* possible to manage mild and passing moods much more easily than we usually think.

Loose Ends

Another issue is likely to come up, especially within the first few days. Obviously it was not possible to include every last person when you did the Deal, and later on you may well think of people you have left out. This can take place in your waking life or even in dreams. You did not consciously exclude these individuals when you did the Deal; they were simply not present in your awareness at that time.

When this happens, imagine the person in front of you and say mentally to him or her, "I forgive you," or "I include you in the Deal as well," or however you want to phrase it. It can be helpful to use some form of visualization in this process—say, imagining the person surrounded by white light or in some other fashion that symbolizes forgiveness in your mind. (People vary enormously in their capacities to visualize, so by all means take into account your strengths and weaknesses here.)

You can do all of this in a few seconds, with only the most minor break in your routine. In some cases, however, it may take longer, and you may have to set aside some time to go through the process of forgiveness with these particular people.

In other cases, you may have included people in the Deal and have genuinely forgiven them at the time, only to have your usual anger and resentment toward them arise again later. Again, this is to some degree a matter of emotional habit: this is the direction in which your mind tends to go. Like a horse that plods unthinkingly down a familiar road, it will continue to head there unless you consciously direct it someplace else.

Morning Guy and Night Guy

There is another reason that these grievances keep surfacing. Gurd-jieff, the spiritual teacher I mentioned earlier, taught that we are not, as we think, one single, unified "I" but a plurality of little "I"s, and each surfaces from time to time, doing things and making promises that other "I"s do not remember or even understand. In this sense, we are all milder versions of what psychologists call multiple personality disorder. "Man is a plurality," said Gurdjieff. "Man's name is legion." One familiar example is the resolution that you might make one evening to get up early the next day and go to the gym for some exercise. The "I" that is dominant in the evening is eager, but the "I" that wakes up the next morning has not the slightest interest in any such program and turns over and goes back to sleep.

Comedian Jerry Seinfeld has a routine about this issue. It's about two battling selves called Morning Guy and Night Guy: "Night Guy wants to stay up late. What about getting up after five hours' sleep? 'Oh, that's Morning Guy's problem. That's not my problem; I'm Night Guy. I stay up as late as I want.' There's nothing Morning Guy can do. The only thing Morning Guy can do is try and oversleep often enough so that Day Guy loses his job and Night Guy has no money to go out anymore."

On a more serious note, we can see this process in times of acute grief, after, say, the loss of a loved one. The first few days are hard, but gradually the pain subsides. Nonetheless, at strange, unbidden moments, the sorrow returns and one begins sobbing again, reminded, perhaps, of the lost person by some item or detail. In these cases, it sometimes seems as if not all the "I"s within oneself learn of the death at the same time, and when they discover it, the grief breaks out again.

In terms of the Deal, it may happen that one "I" makes the resolution to forgive, while any number of other "I"s are simply not aware of it or are even opposed to the idea. To use Seinfeld's language, Morning Guy may have forgiven when Night Guy has done nothing of the kind. This is especially likely to happen when the grievances are long-standing and deep-seated—as with family members, or in instances where you believe that someone has done you great harm.

In these cases, you can again use the technique of letting the grievance drop, mentally saying, "I forgive you" or "I include you in the Deal," or, sometimes, simply thinking about something else. You can also try sending mental blessings in the way described in the previous chapter. The simplest approaches are sometimes the most effective. As one spiritual teacher I knew used to say, "A lighter touch goes deeper."

Even if you feel frustrated by the constant return of these grudges, you may be making more progress than you know. You can think of the process as stripping away layer after layer of anger and resentment until they are all gone.

Backing Off

Granted, there are times when habitual irritation will continue and intense grievances will resurface despite your best efforts. Still more difficult are the cases where even the will to forgive seems to have evaporated: one falls into dark moods of bitterness and aggravation and sees the whole world as a hostile and unforgiving place, and one has completely lost the desire to see it otherwise. Moods like this, triggered by any number of factors, can even last for several days. In that time you may feel that you are very far away from the Deal or have lost it entirely.

There is only so far that you can push yourself in these situations. It would be nice if you could suddenly discard all your gloomy feelings, remember your act of total forgiveness, and see the world bathed in light again. This does not always happen. When it doesn't, a certain amount of patience and discrimination is called for. Usually it's best to avoid fighting with yourself: You are in no mood to think about forgiveness and you are not going to be told you should, by yourself or by anybody else. Being angry with yourself for your refusal to forgive (which will usually be interpreted by the mind as yet another personal failing for which you're supposed to feel guilty) only makes the situation worse. Instead of getting into this internal argument, it's usually wisest to step back from it all and simply allow yourself to be in a bad mood for a while. After all, you are trying to practice total forgiveness, and this must necessarily include yourself. And it must include yourself even and especially when you are feeling at your worst.

While there is a limit beyond which you should not indulge your negative emotions, they do show up and need to be acknowledged for what they are. They must, as it were, be given space to stand and give their performance on the stage of your attention. You don't have to detain them or ask for encores, but trying to get rid of them prematurely will often accomplish nothing at all except to make them stay longer.

In all these situations, it can be helpful to remember one thing: By doing the Deal, you planted a seed of forgiveness inside yourself. If you did it with some degree of sincerity, this seed will stay with you and it will not die. You can forget it and you can cover it over—even, perhaps, for decades—but you are unlikely to lose it entirely. Why? Because the Deal is based on something genuine:

the idea that grievances are useless and harmful and the only way to heal yourself of them is to forgive. This is the truth. Like truth in many other forms and situations, you may fail to see it for a long time, and you may not even like seeing it when you do. But once you have seen it, you can never entirely blind yourself to it again.

To switch metaphors, you can think of the Deal as a kind of thread that has been inserted into the core of your life. You may lose sight of this thread almost completely for a period, but—at least this is my experience—it will, sooner or later, resurface and make its presence felt again within you. This is not to be feared. It is the way out of hell for you.

Constant Presences

Up to now, for the most part I have been talking about forgiveness for the past. You may have hated your sixth-grade schoolteacher, but she is no longer around to trouble you, and you are complaining about her now only in your memory. Forgiveness here is straightforward enough (if not always easy). It's a different matter when the irritations are present and constant. A situation like this might involve a noisy neighbor or a coworker or family member you don't get along with. You may be willing to forgive everything this person has done in the past, but what do you do when he continues to annoy you every day?

The first thing to do is remember that you have chosen to forgive this person. Even if your feelings aren't cooperating, it is a wish that you have made somewhere inside yourself, and this in itself has power. Here it may be wise to bring in what the Hungarian spiritual teacher Georg Kühlewind calls the "soft will" or "gentle will." This will is, he says, "relaxed, receptive, expressive, creative, soft, light, and playful." It is the kind of will one uses when playing music or writing a poem. He contrasts it with the "hard will," the head-on force we use to accomplish something. The soft will is an extremely useful quality to employ when trying to practice forgiveness, since if we try to push ourselves too hard in a given direction, we will experience a backlash.

In dealing with an irritating person, using the soft will might involve ignoring slights, smiling, and saying something friendly if it is possible (and it is not always possible). The inner feeling is light and carefree, the kind of mood that you feel when walking along a sunny path on a pleasant day. You may, as a result, notice some break in the impasse, some room in which you both can function more freely and fluidly.

If you still find it hard to forgive, something else could be going on. You could feel that some border is being crossed, some transgression is being made on your person or your territory. People can be quite clever about this: I once knew a man who liked to irritate his neighbors by parking his car just at the edge of their driveway—not enough to get his car ticketed, but certainly enough to be annoying.

This raises an issue that frequently lurks in the background. Forgiveness is blocked by the fear that you will become a doormat— that if you let your guard down, other people will rush to trample you. Clearly this happens in human relations, so the concern is far from irrational. But it might be wise to remember, in the first place, that your grievances are not a good defense (after all, the person who gets angry in the game of annoyances is the loser), and, in the second place, that you can forgive while still standing your ground.

The Jewish mystical tradition known as the Kabbalah speaks of two forces that need to be kept in balance. The Hebrew words for them are *hesed* and *gevurah*, which can be translated as "mercy" and "severity," respectively. The merciful aspect of our natures is generous, giving, and indulgent. In this Jewish tradition, this quality is represented by the patriarch Abraham, who was said to leave the flaps of his tent open in all four directions so he could welcome travelers no matter where they were coming from. *Gevurah*, on the other hand, is the ability to draw the line, to say "This stops *here*." Keeping these in balance is crucial to any mature and decent life.

To take one example that will be familiar to city dwellers: You have a neighbor who plays his stereo too loud. At first you probably use the quality of mercy—simply allowing it to go on because you don't want to pick a fight and you hope the noise will stop soon anyway. But if it doesn't, you will probably reach a point at which you say "Enough!" and ask the neighbor to turn the stereo down. This is *gevurah*.

You can easily see how these forces can become out of balance. If you are too merciful, you let the music blare for hours, and you grow more and more nervous or simply leave the house. Or the pendulum may swing in the other direction, and you go over and shout at your neighbor—too much severity. But most people are likely to let the music go on for a little bit and then finally ask for some quiet—a reasonable balance between the two qualities.

I bring this up because forgiveness is frequently associated with too much of what I have called mercy—in this case, simply putting up with the annoyance. Personally, I don't see it that way. I think it is perfectly consistent with using the gentle will to assert yourself politely but firmly. This is almost certainly the way to deal with the problem without creating too much trouble for yourself or anyone else.

Like everything, this approach doesn't always work. I had to deal with it myself a number of years ago. My neighbors had a rock 'n' roll band that would rehearse at a murderous volume every Saturday afternoon. I asked them to stop (as graciously as I could) and eventually they did (as ungraciously as they could). But then they got a dog that jumped up on their roof and barked at everything it saw, so I had to ask them to deal with that as well. After a certain point it was obvious that they took pleasure from spiting me, and no reconciliation was possible. It wasn't the only reason I moved a few months afterward, but it was certainly one of them. I have to admit that forgiveness came only later.

Although, as we've established, I'm not much of a salesman, I seem to have pulled a classic bait-and-switch ploy. I started by offering what looked like a simplistic quickie solution but what in the end looks more like a long-term, demanding, and sometimes difficult discipline. If I were so charged, I would have to plead guilty. All the same, ridding yourself of grievances is no small blessing.

The things I've discussed in this chapter seem to me some of the most common and likely issues that may come up after doing the Deal. Certainly there are many more. Next I'll try to deal with a few of them in question-and-answer form.

5

QUESTIONS AND CONCERNS

What is your own personal experience with the Deal?

My experience starts with an encounter with a remarkable text known as *A Course in Miracles*. It is by any account an unusual book. It was channeled—that is, transmitted mentally—to a New York psychologist named Helen Schucman. At one point in 1965 she heard an inner voice that said, "This is a course in miracles. Please take notes." Even more remarkably, this voice claimed to be that of Jesus Christ.

Disturbed by this alien presence in her psyche, she spoke to a colleague named Bill Thetford, wondering whether she was becoming schizophrenic. Since, as he pointed out, she did not show any symptoms of schizophrenia, this was unlikely. She asked what she ought to do. He advised her to do what the voice said—take notes.

This was the beginning of a process that took several years, in which Schucman heard this voice dictating its course in miracles. She had some control over the process—the voice would stop when she was interrupted or chose to stop for the time being—but if she neglected the task for any great amount of time, she would grow uncomfortable.

In the end, this process of mental dictation, allegedly by the founder of Christianity, produced a 1,200-page work consisting of a Text; a Workbook (with 365 lessons to be practiced, one each day for a year); and a Teacher's Manual. The book was privately published in 1975, and, almost completely by word of mouth, it has sold two million copies since then.

A Course in Miracles sets out a radical revision of Christianity, in which love is the only reality and forgiveness the task of everyone on earth. I won't go into the Course's elaborate theoretical system here, but forgiveness is certainly among its central themes. The daily lessons in the Workbook have titles such as "Forgiveness is my function as the light of the world," "Forgiveness is the key to happiness," and "Forgiveness offers everything I want."

Was *A Course in Miracles* really dictated by the voice of Jesus Christ? There is no way of settling this question one way or another. Schucman, who was an atheist (at least at the start of the process), never sought to profit from the Course, avoided publicity, and in fact seemed uncomfortable with her creation, so she was probably not a fraud. The Course is an eloquent work—much of its prose scans as blank verse—and its theological system is extraordinarily clear, consistent, and powerful, but that proves nothing one way or the other. Certainly the ideas in the Course differ—sometimes radically—from those propounded in the New Testament, but even this doesn't tell us much: most mainstream scholars agree that Jesus did not say or do many of the things the Gospels say he did.

To speak personally, I would agree with the man who said that the Course is only sacred text whose native language is English. It would be a spiritual masterpiece whether it had been channeled by Jesus Christ or pounded out by a roomful of chimps banging on keyboards.

I first learned about the Course in September 1980, when I was taking a plane to move to San Francisco. At the airport I bought a copy of *Psychology Today* magazine to read on the flight. This issue contained an article titled "The Gospel According to Helen," which discussed the Course and its growing popularity. I thought the piece was interesting, but didn't think any more about it until several months later, when I found a set of the Course (it was originally published in three volumes, though current editions include all three parts in one volume) in a used bookstore.

I happened to be in a dejected mood that day, having learned that I was not going to get a job that I'd been counting on, so to cheer myself up I bought the books, mostly as a curiosity. I took them home and started reading them. I found the text rather impenetrable, but the workbook lessons seemed straightforward enough, so I started to do them, and continued for a year until I was done.

About six months into the Course, I decided to see if there were any groups that met to discuss it. I called the Foundation for Inner Peace, the books' publisher, and was told that there was a group in San Francisco's Haight-Ashbury district. I went, and found that despite the setting, the people in the group were not very hippielike. They were mostly quiet, middle-aged professionals, and the woman who led it had been trained as an Adlerian psychotherapist. I never met Helen Schucman, who died in 1981, the year I started doing the Course, although I did meet her colleague Bill Thetford once or twice at a group that met in Tiburon, across the bay from San Francisco. He struck me as an extremely pleasant and unobtrusive man who made absolutely no attempt to puff himself up over his connection with the Course; he did not even lead the group at which I met him. He died in 1988.

For more than thirty years, I have worked with the Course and tried to live by its principles (although I have studied other traditions as well). I've tried to practice forgiveness as much as possible, although, as my comments in the previous chapter may suggest, this has not always been easy or gone well.

So this is part of the background, but as a matter of fact the Course does not saying anything about a Deal. Nor have I used the Course's intricate theoretical system while discussing forgiveness here, for reasons that are too complicated for me to go into at present.

The Deal itself came to me much later. At this point I had been under some strain for several years because of the challenges of working and having my wife work as we were raising two small sons. The salaries we earned—we were both employed by the same nonprofit organization—were not enough to keep us from continual financial concerns, nor was the small amount I was able to make doing freelance projects.

The strain grew especially intense when, after much soul searching, my wife felt that she could no longer work at that job and quit abruptly and surprisingly (to everyone but me). Although this had been coming for some time, we had made no plans for the aftermath and were plunged into still more worries about money. We had been struggling to keep things going simply to pay our mortgage and various debts that had accrued over the years. It was complicated further by the fact that I was still working at the same place and of course did not feel terribly warm toward my colleagues.

I grew increasingly nervous and distraught; I seemed to be encircled by a fence of family responsibilities and financial limitations. Then, at some point a couple of weeks later, I made a decision within myself to simply forgive everything and to ask forgiveness for everything in return. Although I had done this in various ways before, it had never been so complete or so final.

After that I felt the burden had lifted. On the face of it nothing had changed. But I was willing to let go of my grievances against my coworkers and everyone else and to forgive the situation as well. Everything was not suddenly made easy, and our difficulties did not vanish, but at any rate it was possible to go on.

For the first days afterward, I felt unusually calm, serene, and euphoric, and even had a burst of creative energy. My mood was sunnier than it had been in years. Over the next day or so, the idea of the Deal began to germinate, first as the topic for a workshop presentation, then as a book.

After about a week, though, I went through a sharp backlash and fell into a period of irritation, anger, and withdrawal. My complaints against the world returned in full force, and my situation seemed black as ever. The whole idea of the Deal fell far to the back of my mind, and I didn't feel much connection with it. Nor was I in any mood to force myself into a positive frame of mind. The best I could do was keep some memory of the Deal—some thread—alive, so that even if I didn't have access to feelings of love and forgiveness, I hadn't entirely turned my back on them.

This experience illustrates a principle that seems to be present at many levels in the universe—what some have called the law of rhythm. The pendulum swings, and then it swings back in the opposite direction. We take this into account in the physical world, but not always in the psychological world. Nevertheless it seems to operate there too in some strangely similar way. A wave of hatred is followed by a backlash of sympathy; a hero or celebrity is put on a high pedestal, only to be rudely removed soon thereafter.

So it is with forgiveness, and I think we need to reckon with this in our inner lives. It's quite possible that, having done the Deal, you may feel warmth and compassion toward someone you previously disliked, only to have the tide swing the other way in a day or so. This does not mean that you have failed to forgive or that forgiveness is nonsense. It does mean that your emotions have their own rhythms and dynamics, and if you recognize this fact, they will cause you less pain, or at any rate less bewilderment. Eventually they will settle into equilibrium.

This dark phase of mine lasted for something less than a week. It broke one evening as suddenly as it had come, and the stimulus for the change was as small and insignificant as the one that had put me into such a dark mood (in fact, I don't remember what it was in either case). From that point on, my mood improved, and although it did not quite return to the euphoria I had felt at first, it was more stable and balanced.

Although my personal circumstances after that point were still as difficult as they had been for a long time in my life, I was able to maintain mental and emotional equilibrium with much greater ease.

How can you even talk about forgiveness when the world is the way it is?

It's *because* the world is the way it is that I talk about forgiveness. It seems to me that the world is the way it is because of a radical lack of forgiveness, and this is one reason I've chosen to write this book.

Christ said, "Resist not evil." Many people, on the other hand, assume that it is only weakness that allows evil to flourish, and that if everyone rose up at once and opposed evil, it would be destroyed forever. Maybe, but this is not likely. It *might* be possible, if everyone were to rise up and fight the *same* evil—and if this were at the same time a *genuine* evil—but this never happens. Instead people oppose evil as it appears to them—a matter about which they never agree and about which they are often wrong. If you look back at the horrors of the twentieth century, you will see that they all started as ways of opposing evil as it appeared to a particular group of people.

In fact, history might have something to teach us about the value of forgiveness. If you were to give an account of human hatred and vindictiveness, you would more or less have to write a history of the world. If you were to write a history of forgiveness, you would have far fewer things to choose from. Still, a few can be found.

We might, for example, turn to Lincoln's second inaugural address, delivered when the forces of the Union were about to crush the South. The magnanimity he shows in the speech is especially remarkable when we consider not only the enormous quantities of blood that had been shed over the previous four years, but the vitriolic hatred that had been directed at Lincoln personally. Toward the end of his speech are two of the most resonant phrases in American history: "With malice toward none, with charity toward all." Historians suppose that Lincoln would have shown the same mercy toward the defeated South, but he was shot a few weeks later, and his successors took a much harsher course—and, one could argue, we in the United States are still paying for it.

We could then look at the greatest events of the twentieth century—the two world wars. Both ended with the defeat of Germany, but the aftermaths were quite different. In World War I, the British navy imposed a blockade against Germany, and British naval power made this blockade an extraordinarily successful one. As a result, hundreds of thousands of German civilians starved to death. Astonishingly, however, the British continued the blockade for eight months *after* Germany's surrender, and in fact this was later considered to be the time of the blockade's most devastating effects.

The blockade was sustained to make sure that Germany signed the humiliating Treaty of Versailles, which it did in June 1919. By this it agreed to accept full responsibility for the war, concede major territories, and pay 132 billion marks in reparations to the Allies.

The Treaty of Versailles was meant to teach Germany a lesson, but it didn't work. Twenty years later, a much more powerful and malevolent Germany started World War II. It took the forces of almost the entire rest of the world to defeat Germany and the other Axis powers.

After this war, however, the victorious Allies, led by the United States, helped its defeated enemies—Germany, Japan, and Italy—to rebuild. Instead of demanding billions in reparations, the United States provided billions in aid. This act of forgiveness— which was all the more remarkable because the defeated nations had committed some of the most terrible atrocities in history—permitted the nations of the former Axis to reenter the world community. Today, seventy years later, there are many threats to world peace, but these nations are not high among them.

Still more recently, the South African government, after the end of apartheid in the early 1990s, instituted the Truth and Reconciliation Commission to hear the complaints of victims as well as requests for amnesty by perpetrators. According to most accounts, the commission brought about a much more peaceful transition than many had feared, and it has been imitated in other countries. South Africa today may not be a model society, but the bloodbath that had been forecast as a sequel to apartheid did not take place.

I bring up these historical examples because they illustrate on a large scale what forgiveness may accomplish. Forgiveness, often derided as foolish and naive, particularly in terms of realpolitik, seems in many cases to be the more prudent route.

Some may respond by saying, for example, that the United States after World War II was motivated by self-interest. That may be so—but then one of the central points of this book is that forgiveness *is* a matter of self-interest.

My therapist says I need to get in touch with my anger, and I'm afraid that the Deal will get in the way of this process.

Although I'm not a psychologist, the theory seems to go like this: Surface problems such as anxiety and depression sometimes serve as masks for more deep-seated issues. These issues often reflect traumas from the past—particularly childhood. They were too painful to deal with at the time, so the conscious ego closed itself off from them—meaning that they still go unnoticed and untreated well into adult life.

The purpose of many kinds of psychotherapy is to help the client get in touch with the feelings that are underlying the symptoms on the surface. Because these are painful feelings, the conscious mind tends to turn away from them, but this is like ignoring a wound that needs to be cleansed and bandaged; it will only fester and grow worse.

Often these feelings include anger. Getting in touch with your anger, then, is a way of having the conscious mind acknowledge these feelings and experience them fully. It then becomes possible to let them go. This is not always easy and it does not always happen quickly, but if the therapy proceeds as it should, it usually produces some kind of emotional release. This is perhaps why every therapist's office has a box of tissues prominently displayed.

In any event, the ultimate goal of getting in touch with your anger is to let it go and move on with your life. This is perfectly consistent with the Deal, even if it means that you appear to be putting off forgiveness for a certain amount of time.

I've read that one of our problems today is that we deny our own dark sides and try to make ourselves completely good. Isn't the Deal a way of denying our dark sides?

This idea rests on a profound insight—that frequently we only see what we want to see of ourselves and blind ourselves to our weaker and more repellent aspects.

The Deal doesn't contradict this approach. It does not call upon you to deny or ignore the parts of yourself that you are ashamed of, or even the parts that may be genuinely bad. (Anyone who can't see evil in himself is blind.) In fact, the Deal urges you to be aware of all the parts of yourself, those you like and those you don't like, and forgive them equally.

Will the Deal help me reach enlightenment?

Enlightenment, in the sense most often used today, is a fairly new concept in the West. It has been imported from Eastern traditions, particularly Hinduism and Buddhism.

The idea of enlightenment, as popularly understood, is a rather vague one, and the hearsay about it does not help us reach much clarity. Sometimes enlightenment appears to be a moment of awakening that makes it impossible to be anything other than totally illuminated from that point on. People who have had this kind of awakening are perfect or very nearly so, beyond all error or evil. If they have students, they are incapable of harming them; any supposedly harsh treatment is really just another form of teaching.

And some of these teachers have behaved very harshly indeed. There is a point beyond which this kind of behavior can't be excused as a form of teaching.

Recently I was on a TV talk show with Jay Michaelson, author of *Evolving Dharma: Meditation, Buddhism, and the Next Generation of Enlightenment.* He raised a point that has troubled many people: There are a number of supposedly enlightened beings around—but they don't always behave in ways that seem enlightened. Jay said he even knew of Zen masters who had certificates of enlightenment but still abused their students. (I don't know what a certificate of enlightenment looks like, but I would love to have one.)

This kind of behavior is certainly not limited to Buddhism or Hinduism. Nevertheless, it has been common enough that the word *guru* has been turned into a kind of slur, making the whole concept of enlightenment seem absurd.

At one point I decided to ask my good friend John Cianciosi, author of *The Meditative Path* and a former Buddhist monk himself, exactly what enlightenment is supposed to be. He said that according to the traditional Buddhist scriptures, an enlightened being is one in whom the Three Poisons—desire, anger, and obliviousness—have been completely eradicated.

This explains a great deal. It means that having an intense experience of illumination—which many people have had—is not in and of itself enough to make you an enlightened being. Apparently a much longer and more rigorous purification of the soul is necessary.

Certainly I am nowhere near being enlightened, and I have never met anyone who was. So it's impossible for me to say whether the Deal will help you reach enlightenment.

If I were to guess, however, I would say that the Deal would be more likely to lead you toward enlightenment than away from it.

I believe that forgiveness comes only from faith in Jesus Christ.

Then by all means ask forgiveness of Jesus. You will notice that I explicitly mentioned that possibility in the instructions for the Deal.

But another assumption may be lurking in the background. You may be thinking that no one can be forgiven except through faith in Jesus, and that is certainly the doctrine of much of Christianity.

I don't agree with this teaching, and this is why.

Let's set aside the often-mentioned example of "savages" in the jungle who have never heard of Jesus and therefore will never have the chance to be saved. Let's take another case closer to home.

I have a friend who was raised as an Orthodox Jew. When he was a boy, he said, every day on the way home from school the Irish kids beat him up for being a Jew. What kind of associations would you expect him to have with Christ or Christianity? He could hardly be expected to go down on his knees and beg salvation from someone in whose name he suffered so much hurt. "All I know," he once told me, "was I got into a lot of trouble because of *that* rabbi."

Conservative Christians may reply that this may be unfortunate, but nonetheless it is the will of God. But there is a logical problem here. Christianity also teaches that God is infinitely more merciful and compassionate than any human being can be or even imagine. But I, who am probably a person of middling compassion, would never make someone fry in hell for eternity because he had been beaten up in the name of someone who was supposed to save him. This strikes me as extraordinarily cruel.

So we have a situation in which an infinitely merciful God behaves in a way that is more vindictive than that of an ordinary human being. This is logically absurd, and no invocation of "mysteries" or "the inscrutable will of God" is going to get around it.

Thus I believe that forgiveness can be offered and received in a much wider range of contexts than many religions teach.

The conclusion is this: If you feel the need to ask and offer forgiveness in the name of Jesus, this is certainly consistent with the Deal. But don't assume that everyone has to go the same route as you.

Do you believe that there is such a thing as evil in the world, and if so, what does forgiveness have to do with it?

This question itself, which is commonly asked in one form or another, reveals an interesting assumption about the nature of reality. People often ask questions such as "Is evil real?" or "Why does evil exist?" But they almost never ask if good is real, or why goodness should exist.

This fact tells us something important. Deep within us, we believe that the universe is fundamentally good, and that evil is in some way a secondary phenomenon.

In any event, to ask whether evil is real in some metaphysical sense is fascinating, but it doesn't seem to apply much to life as we know it. Some say that evil is illusory, but it still *feels* real. You, like me and everyone else, have as palpable a sense of suffering as you do of joy.

I have explored the problem of evil at some length in chapter 9 of my book *Inner Christianity*, and I won't repeat the discussion here. But it is worth asking how forgiveness relates to evil.

Let's begin with the notion of the personal Devil as conventional Christianity portrays him. The Devil, or Satan, does not actually appear very often in the Bible. When he does, he is not an enemy of God but rather a kind of quality-control officer. He asks God if he can test Job to see if he really is a good man, and he tempts Christ in the wilderness for much the same reason.

The name of the Devil tells us something about his function. It comes from the Greek *diabolos*, which means "accuser." This makes perfect sense in the light of his function in the biblical stories. He's like a district attorney—except that he's a district attorney who also has the right and duty to tempt the suspect to commit the crime.

However literally or metaphorically you want to take this, the Devil clearly has to do with accusation. His other name, Satan, is Hebrew for "opponent." In Goethe's drama *Faust*, when Faust first meets the devil Mephistopheles, he asks who he is. Mephistopheles replies, "I am the spirit who always denies."

Accusation, opposition, denial—these are central concepts associated with the Devil. They are also the diametric opposite of forgiveness. To forgive is not to accuse or oppose. It is to accept another person rather than deny her.

It has sometimes been said that nearness and distance in the spiritual world work by a different set of principles than they do in the physical world. In the spiritual realm there is no such thing as physical proximity, because there is no such thing as space. Hence you cannot be physically close to, or far from, God. Rather, in the spiritual world, nearness is based upon similarity. The more you are like God, the closer you are to him. The more you are like the Devil, the closer you are to him.

Thus if you want to avoid evil, you would move away from accusation toward forgiveness.

I don't believe in God, and I don't believe in karma either. So why should I do the Deal?

Ironically, in that case you might want to do the Deal *because of* the price you have to pay—the grudges and grievances that you give up. Even if there is no God and no karma, you will benefit enormously from unloading all of these resentments. That is reason enough.

I still say there are some things that shouldn't be forgiven.

This brings up an extremely important issue that often serves as a block to forgiveness. It has to do with the difference between forgiving and condoning. People often assume that to forgive something is to condone it, and this is something they are (sometimes rightly) unwilling to do.

I can best explain my thoughts about this with a story about something that happened to me when I was an undergraduate. It developed that a good friend of mine wanted to have an affair with my girlfriend. My girlfriend was interested, but she had enough of a conscience to ask me first if this was all right with me.

It wasn't all right with me, and I said so. The news immediately got back to my friend, and I found him waiting to talk to me after a class one day. He was extremely apologetic. I wasn't particularly pleasant to him, and after we walked together for a few minutes we separated without any reconciliation.

Although I was angry with my girlfriend too, I had to accept that nothing had actually happened between them (at least to my knowledge), and I decided to let the whole thing go. Our relationship lasted for another five years.

It took a few weeks, but in the end I decided to drop my anger against my friend as well. Little by little we took up where we had left off, and soon our friendship continued much as it had before. As far as I can tell, he never tried to sleep with my girlfriend again, and we all remained friends for a long time afterward.

In all honesty, I can't say how I would have responded had they actually had an affair. Maybe I would have been able to forgive, and maybe I wouldn't. I wasn't practicing forgiveness in any conscious way, so practically anything might have happened.

In any case, I couldn't condone the affair. I couldn't just let it happen. That, to my mind, would have been weakness. Forgiveness doesn't mean letting people trample on you. But having stopped the affair, in the long run I couldn't see any point in clinging to resentments about it. So I can honestly say that in this situation I was able to forgive without condoning.

We often hear the expression "Forgive and forget." I don't think this is necessarily a good idea. I may have forgiven, but I have remembered the incident well enough to talk about it thirty-five years later.

Your example is about a comparatively small thing. What about big things like rape and murder? Should they be forgiven?

The question then becomes, forgiven by whom? By you? By me? By the powers that be? By society at large?

If the crime directly involves you, admittedly it can be a hard situation. You crave justice, but sometimes this justice ends up looking very much like revenge.

In 1808 the German author Heinrich von Kleist wrote a short novel around this theme; titled *Michael Kohlhaas*, it is set in sixteenth-century Germany. Michael Kohlhaas is a horse dealer who has a couple of his horses confiscated by a petty nobleman as he is passing through the nobleman's domain. The horses are returned later, but in poor condition, and Kohlhaas's servant, who stayed behind to tend them, has been beaten. Kohlhaas seeks redress, first from the nobleman and then from higher authorities, but he is refused. Enraged, Kohlhaas wages a vendetta on the nobleman, leading a private army to attack him and burn down his castle. Finally Kohlhaas is arrested as a threat to civil order and executed.

The theme of this novella is a hunger for justice that surpasses all bounds. Aristotle taught that virtue is a mean between two extremes, and that any virtue, when taken to an extreme, becomes a vice. Michael Kohlhaas is a man in whom the thirst for justice has become a cancer.

Although *Michael Kohlhaas* is based on a true story, let's now take a counterexample from real life. In 1977, the film director Roman Polanski sexually molested a thirteen-year-old girl named Samantha Geimer. Polanski fled the United States and has remained out of the country since, preventing him from facing criminal charges. (He was arrested in Switzerland in 2009, but he was not extradited to the United States and was later released.) Although Geimer did win a civil suit against Polanski in 1988, since then she has publicly proclaimed a message of "enough is enough," and in 2003, when Polanski was nominated for an

Academy Award for his film *The Pianist*, she even published an opinion piece entitled "Judge the Movie, Not the Man."

Should Samantha Geimer be held up as a model of forgiveness? Maybe, maybe not. But she probably chose the wisest course by leaving the past behind her—at least as much as is possible in such a highly publicized circumstance.

So, then, are you saying that society should forgive these crimes? What would happen if all crimes were suddenly forgiven?

Here I have to admit that I've conceived of the Deal as something to be done by individuals, or at most by groups. It's not clear to me how it would apply to society at large. But let's try to see where this possibility might take us.

One of the most famous statements in moral philosophy is the categorical imperative of Immanuel Kant: "Act only according to that maxim whereby you can, at the same time, will that it should become a universal law." To put it more simply, why should you love your neighbor? Because everyone should love his neighbor. Why should you avoid murder? Because everyone should avoid murder.

Let's take this idea and apply it to the Deal: What if everyone on earth were to wake up tomorrow and decide to forgive totally? Would the world be a better place or a worse place? I venture to guess that it would be better.

If this happened, of course it might transpire that the prison doors would open and murderers and rapists would go free. But then, since everyone would be practicing total forgiveness—including criminals—it might also transpire that there were no more rapes or murders.

So, then, we have two choices:

1. Murderers and rapists are punished, and murders and rapes continue.
2. Murderers and rapists are forgiven, and murders and rapes stop.

Which would you prefer?

These are, of course, all-or-nothing cases, and they are very unlikely to come about in real life. In any case, you may reply, the world is not like that. People take advantage. Sometimes forgiving turns out to be condoning.

And, of course, you would be right.

So I frankly have to say that I don't know what a society based on forgiveness would really look like. (For some seventeen hundred years, Western civilization has paid lip service to this ideal, but we don't seem to have moved very far toward it.) The art and science of forgiveness are primitive and practically undeveloped. I can dimly imagine only a psychology of forgiveness, a sociology of forgiveness, or a jurisprudence of forgiveness. I would guess that if such things were ever to evolve in the future, people would look back and regard this book (if they remembered it at all) somewhat as an art critic today regards a palm print smeared in red ochre on the wall of a cave.

Nevertheless, it is almost universally agreed that the criminal justice system in America is a shambles and accomplishes nothing, except, perhaps, to keep offenders off the streets for a limited time. So we are hardly trying to fix something that isn't broken. In fact, the current system is so badly broken that no one can quite agree on how to fix it.

So it's true that I have no clear social model to offer, but this in itself shouldn't close off the idea of forgiveness on a large scale. All social constructs are necessarily the product of masses of people working over the course of years and even centuries, and a true civilization of forgiveness would take generations to build and would lead us in directions that I can scarcely dream of. That I can't sit down and conjure up a utopia of forgiveness means nothing. Besides, we have had plenty of descriptions of utopias, and they are for the most part worthwhile only as entertainment.

Why did you mention celebrities in the Deal?

Although current society is intensely fascinated by celebrities, the role they actually play in our culture doesn't seem to be well understood.

To begin with, we live in a society of strangers. We are no longer tribespeople or villagers whose acquaintance totals a few dozen people. Every day we see and deal with many individuals we will never see again. This is especially true in big cities and suburbs.

Even people we see every day are, more or less, strangers to us. How much do you know about the people you work with? Do you and they have any common acquaintances outside of the workplace? What about your neighbors? I've lived for five years in the same middle-class suburb on the edges of the Chicago metropolis. I know some of my neighbors, a couple of them quite well, but the vast majority of those who live around me are people I don't know and probably wouldn't recognize in most settings.

At the same time, we find ourselves interacting with these

strangers in various ways, and we have to talk to them about something. One thing we all share is a familiarity with certain famous people—politicians, movie stars, singers, sports heroes, and so on. These celebrities furnish a kind of common acquaintance that we can talk about with people with whom we otherwise have little to share.

But we have a very curious attitude toward these celebrities. We like to build them up and then tear them down again. Often they let themselves in for it by doing stupid, bizarre, or criminal things, but the vehemence we show (while enormous atrocities elsewhere in the world are attracting little notice) suggests that something else is going on. In part it may be a matter of envy. We live in a democratic, egalitarian society, where nobody is any better than anybody else (or so we tell ourselves). At the same time we want to have heroes to admire and look up to. These impulses are somewhat contradictory, and so it's no surprise that they produce contradictory results—elevating the star, then tearing her down.

When you think about it, however, even the celebrity you most abhor is in all likelihood someone who has never harmed you personally, if only because she has never met you. You may have even seen her in movies and shows and realized that, as a matter of fact, you have had nothing but pleasure from her performances. But because she has cheated on a lover or has been caught driving drunk, you get satisfaction from despising her. You may even start to feel sincerely angry with her.

In part, this whole phenomenon is a way of cementing common values: to malign a celebrity who abuses drugs is, or seems to be, a way of condemning drug abuse as a whole. But the hatred that is sometimes directed at famous people seems to be out of all proportion to anything they have done. Many of them have harmed no one but themselves.

To my mind, hostility toward public figures, for any reason, doesn't jibe with an attitude of forgiveness. At best it's a way of displacing your anger onto some remote object. But it would make more sense to see what it is in your own life you're angry about and take steps to remedy it—or at least forgive the situation if there is nothing else you can do.

I am an alcoholic, and I'm still drinking. Can I still do the Deal?

Absolutely. You'll notice that there are no prerequisites for doing the Deal. The only requirements are that you are willing to forgive and be forgiven.

This is not a twelve-step program, nor is it aimed at recovery from substance abuse. I have no experience in these areas, and anything I could say about them would be mere speculation. Helping others recover from drinking or drug use is best left to people who know what they're doing—who often are those who have had to overcome these problems themselves.

In a sense, the Deal doesn't change the situation much when it comes to substance abuse. If you are an addict, you will in all likelihood have to find a way out of your predicament whether you have ever heard of the Deal or not.

All that said, the Deal could be helpful in recovery. In the first place, people usually abuse drugs because they are in some kind of pain. You'll notice that most of the commonly abused drugs, including alcohol, cocaine, and opiates, are painkillers. While people sometimes become addicted to these substances as a result of physical pain, they're often trying to drown out emotional pain as well. And this pain has a great deal to do with grievances, resentments, hurts past and present—in short, everything the Deal is asking you to release.

In the second place, the Deal can help you with guilt. Much of our (usually unconscious) thinking about guilt seems to run along these lines: Society needs to ensure that its members behave. It's impossible to station a policeman next to every person to enforce good behavior (although some nations have tried). As a result, we have, since our earliest years, had a kind of inner policeman installed in us called the conscience. This conscience punishes us with feelings of guilt when we have done wrong, and thus it serves as a kind of interior monitor to make sure we behave when no one is looking.

The conscience may serve a purpose when it works this way, but it can also malfunction. A person does something he feels guilty about; his conscience punishes him. He can then unconsciously conclude that he has paid the price for his bad deed, and so is free to do it again. The guilt then becomes a means of enabling bad behavior rather than discouraging it. It can also lead to feelings of unworthiness, degradation, and vileness, creating a self-image of failure that the addict then lives out.

If what I am saying is right, even to a small degree, self-forgiveness may enable an addict to break free of the cycle of self-reinforcing guilt, which could help in recovery. Thus, while the Deal will not necessarily make recovery easier, it may help uproot some of the underlying causes of substance abuse.

One word of caution: If you are involved in a recovery program, I would not suggest dropping out of it and doing the Deal as a supposedly easier alternative. This could quickly turn into a form of avoidance. If you are doing the Twelve Steps or something similar, you can certainly do the Deal as well, but I wouldn't recommend it in place of an actual program for recovery.

*I have a lot of guilt around food and eating, and I have
trouble forgiving myself for it.*

Many people do. Guilt about food pervades American society.
There are very few things that you can eat or drink that can't in
some way make you feel guilty. Sugar is bad for you. So is fat.
Meat is laden with cholesterol. Fruits and vegetables are contami-
nated with pesticides. The list goes on and on.

Many people also feel guilty about being fat, and many people
are fat. The obesity rate among U.S. adults went from 13 percent in
1962 to 35.7 percent in 2010, according to the Centers for Disease
Control. I personally wonder if this rise has something to do with
the decline in smoking. According to the American Lung Associa-
tion, in 1965, 42.5 percent of adults smoked; this fell to 20.6 percent
in 2009. Could it be that over this time many Americans have been
switching their means of oral gratification from tobacco to food?

Whether or not this is so, it may be helpful to look a little bit
deeper into our needs for gratification so that we can forgive ourselves more readily. The psychologist Abraham Maslow created a
famous "hierarchy of needs" in human beings. There are several
layers, and the lower ones at the bottom have to be met first; once
they are, your concern moves up the pyramid to the others.

MASLOW'S HIERARCHY OF NEEDS

Self-actualization

Esteem

Love and Belonging

Security

Physical Needs

At the bottom are basic physical needs including food, clothing, and shelter. If these needs aren't met, you are not going to care about much else. As was once said, "A man may have many problems. A man who has no bread has only one."

Once these basic needs are met, one wants security and safety. After these are assured, social needs come into play. People have needs for family, love, affection, and closeness. They also need the esteem of others; all of us do.

Finally, at the top is self-actualization, which includes things such as creativity, spontaneity, and meaning in life. The need for this is only felt when all the other, more basic needs are met.

Maslow's hierarchy of needs is very ingenious and elegant, and it has been extremely influential. One thing about it that is not so well known, however, is that people who feel deficient in one need will often try to satisfy themselves by overindulging in another. A woman may feel bad about her body, so she overeats: feeling a lack of esteem, she compensates by taking in more food. But all the food in the world won't meet her need for esteem, just as all the carbohydrates in the world won't meet your need for protein. In fact, the fatter she gets, the more her self-esteem will suffer, perpetuating the cycle.

Some of what I've said above about guilt and substance abuse may apply to food as well. You feel guilty for eating too much; you feel punished by the guilt; thus, having satisfied your own need for retribution, you feel free to repeat the activity. This is the essence of self-defeating behavior.

Of course, the answer, again, is forgiveness. I wonder if it's possible to break a habit of compulsive overeating by ceasing to feel guilty about it—by forgiving yourself for overeating. In this way you break the cycle of transgression and guilt followed by further transgression. In any event, the guilt serves no positive purpose. If you release it in an act of self-forgiveness, you can see your own situation more clearly and take the necessary steps.

On another matter: there are many voices today that are trying to make you feel guilty about your choices in food, particularly about eating meat. I personally disagree with this. You may or may not decide to eat meat; that's obviously your choice. But as a matter of fact, people have always eaten meat, and they probably always will, and no amount of sermonizing is going to change this.

Besides, it strikes me as foolish to preach the same diet for everyone. People's needs and tolerances for food vary enormously, and I believe your diet should be decided by things such as your health and your budget as well as your own personal ethics. You may decide to be a vegan or vegetarian; that's up to you. But I don't think it's a good idea to indulge in guilt-mongering to others about the choices they have made.

What does the Deal have to do with sex?

The Deal says nothing specifically about sex. It's open to anyone regardless of sexual preferences, orientation, or practices. Again, you are asked only to forgive and be forgiven. Whatever changes you need to make in your behavior are for you to determine.

Even so, it may be interesting to look a little more deeply into the question of sex. It is the most powerful force to which human beings have access. This may sound surprising in an age of nuclear power, but it's still true. That's because sex is the only force we possess that can create life.

We all know the facts of life, so I don't have to discuss them here. It's not as well-known that sex can be transformed into emotional energy. Probably the most common example is when chills run up the spine.

When, after all, do we feel these chills? Sometimes in moments of fright, sometimes in response to a powerful piece of art or music. In each case we feel some energy running up from the base of the spine, usually to halfway up the back but occasionally even to the head. Possibly in these experiences, you are transmitting vital—that is, sexual—energy, felt in the lower part of the body, into some kind of emotional energy, such as courage, awe, or inspiration, usually felt in the chest.

The mystical literature of the world acknowledges this fact and discusses it in (often deliberately) obscure terms. In Eastern mysticism, for example, you will occasionally read about the awakening of kundalini. Kundalini is said to be a force at the base of the spine that can be sent up to the head by certain esoteric techniques. When this happens in a full-blown form, it's described as a kundalini awakening. It's sometimes practiced to induce mystical illumination, but it's so powerful that it can unhinge an individual. As such, it's only supposed to be done in controlled circumstances and under expert supervision. Chills up the spine are simply the same thing in a much milder form.

The point of saying all this is that, in addition to its other powers, sex can create an energetic bond between individuals. Sometimes this bond is formed directly in the sex act, where the lovers exchange sexual energy (as well as hormones). But sometimes it can happen without any contact at all. It can come on suddenly, almost like a physical blow—hence all the poetry about Cupid's darts and so on. Almost none of this occurs under voluntary control.

This emotional bond doesn't always affect both people in the same way. One may become intensely attached while the other may feel nothing at all. It's usually assumed that the woman feels the bond sooner and more powerfully than the man, but this is far from universal. Moreover, this exchange can happen in any situation, with any number of different results. One or both may be committed to someone else. The relationship may proceed up to a point, and then something happens to break the trust. One or the other may move away. There may be religious or ethnic differences, and so on. It can happen that one person no longer feels the bond while the other one does. Or the relationship may deteriorate to the point where the link is broken, but only with great bitterness.

Novels and films are full of such scenarios, and just about everyone has some personal experience with them as well. The resulting wounds can last a lifetime.

Hence, while doing the Deal, you may want to go back and make sure you release past (and sometimes present) lovers from any bonds that have formed from sexual or emotional energy. As with everything else, it's not terribly helpful to go back and search through motives and reasons and backgrounds. You simply cut through it all and let it go.

In fact, some spiritual traditions (for example, the Hawaiian shamanic path known as *huna*) have described emotional bonds as a kind of invisible sticky cord that links people through desire, affection, or even enmity. If you have a bond like this that you find especially hard to let go of, you might want to visualize this sticky cord going from your solar plexus to that of the other person. Then imagine that you are cutting it off, as an obstetrician cuts an umbilical cord. As with visualization of any kind, you can adapt this image in any way that makes it particularly real or vivid for you. You might have to do this more than once.

I'm cheating on my husband. If I do the Deal, do I have to tell him about the affair and ask his forgiveness?

As I've pointed out, the Deal does not prescribe any specific external actions that you have to perform. Anything you have to do as a result of it is something that you yourself have decided to do.

The reasoning behind this is simple. To begin with, there are already plenty of moral rules. The basic ones don't change, and we all know what they are. There is no reason to add another layer of rules to the many that already exist.

Furthermore, it's difficult, if not impossible, to make universal prescriptions about what a person should or shouldn't do in a given set of circumstances. In some, maybe most, cases, you should tell your husband and ask forgiveness. In others, you may want to break off the affair without telling anyone. In still others, you may want to leave your husband.

Say your husband is an abusive drunkard, and the man you are having an affair with is kind and loving. Or say your husband is cheating as well, and you have an arrangement that is perfectly satisfactory to you both. What should you do then? In the United States, infidelity is universally reviled, but what if you are reading this in France, where it seems to be taken much more lightly?

One could try to apply conventional morality here, but conventional morality doesn't suit every situation.

In this case, the Deal requires you only to forgive your husband, your lover, and yourself. What you may eventually decide to do as a consequence is for you to determine.

I can forgive the people in my life, but I have trouble with the big things—wars, genocides, atrocities. It's very hard to forgive those, and I even wonder if that's the right thing to do.

Let's be clear from the outset: The Deal does not ask you to condone the crimes of humanity, past or present, or to pretend that they didn't happen.

Many people believe that forgiveness means forgetting. As a matter of fact, although this book has talked a lot about forgiveness, it has said nothing about forgetting. It may well be necessary to remember the crimes of history so that they don't happen again. It may even be wise to study the psychology and sociology of these crimes, as some scholars are doing, to understand what in the mind enables people to carry them out.

But to hold on to grievances and pain about these atrocities serves no purpose. Bearing grudges against the villains of history does not punish the villains. Most of them are long dead and (at least in theory) are undergoing whatever retribution they deserve. Your hatred is not going to punish them any further. As for the ones who are still alive, they are almost certainly beyond your reach and are not even aware of your judgments of them. You are not doing them any harm with your feelings. As someone once said, refusing to forgive is like drinking poison and expecting it to hurt someone else.

Even people who have suffered directly from these horrors often find it more beneficial and liberating to put the past behind—however much work that may take—and move on with their lives.

But I feel that someone should speak out against the evils of the world. Otherwise we'll just be letting them continue.

First, some hard news: You are not going to do anything to change the vast majority of evils in the world, now or ever. You simply can't. No one can. There are too many things in the world for any one person to deal with. Even the leaders of great nations have limits to their power.

Let's go further: If you made up your mind to do something

about injustice, what would you do? What if someone dropped you right now in one of the world's trouble spots? Would you be of any use? Or would you just be in the way?

You might feel the need to speak out against injustices, and there are times when this is the right thing to do. But in many cases, people who are speaking out are talking either to those who already agree with them or to those who disagree with them and are not going to change their minds. I'm reminded of this fact almost every time I go on the Internet. It may make some people feel better to vent their hostilities, but it often seems that venting hostilities just fuels more hostilities.

In that case, what kind of positive action can we take?

I would offer two suggestions. In the first place, at the end of the description of the Deal I mentioned the idea of mentally sending blessings and peace to the world as a whole. You can certainly do this for any situation in the world that is troubling you. There is evidence that prayer works, and kind thoughts and feelings may facilitate kind actions or reduce hostile ones. In one case, a group of meditators in Washington, D.C., took part in a study to see if they could reduce the crime rate. They directed their meditation to this end for two months—June and July 1993—and as it turned out, violent crime rates for those months were significantly lower than in the same months during the previous five years.

But say you don't believe in the power of prayer. Even so, sending blessings is a good thing to do, because it occupies your mind with positive thoughts rather than negative ones, and positive thoughts are likely to make you feel better and act more decently toward those around you.

This, I believe, is a useful practice for all the situations in which you have no personal role to play and can do nothing to help materially. And there will be many of these.

But this may still seem rather passive. To do something active in the world is another matter. The answer, I believe, lies in doing your own duty—the function that you were put on this earth to carry out. In India there is a word for this: *svadharma*, which simply means "one's own duty." It is not a moral duty in the ordinary sense; rather, it is the duty that is embedded in your deepest self. No one else can do the job that you were created to do, whatever it is. Your freedom lies not in withdrawing from the world but in performing this duty—which only you can perform. *A Course in Miracles* calls it the special function. It says:

> To each [the Holy Spirit] gives a special function in salvation
> he alone can fill; a part for only him. Nor is the plan complete
> until he finds his special function, and fulfills the part
> assigned to him, to make himself complete within a world
> where incompletion rules ... The Holy Spirit needs your
> special function, that His may be fulfilled. Think not you
> lack a special value here. You wanted it, and it is given you ...
> The form is suited to your special needs, and to the special
> time and place in which you think you find yourself.

How do you find your special function? There is no one single
way. People learn their special functions in many different ways
and at different times of life. One person knows hers from childhood; another discovers it only in middle age. It is revealed by
still, small voices and by visions on the road to Damascus, but
also sometimes in a career aptitude test or by answering an ad in
the classifieds. Your special function may remain the same all
your life, or it may gradually change with circumstances. When
you discover it, you may have the unshakable sense that this function, whatever it is, is why you exist, is what you were created to
do. But it may not be so. It may feel instead as if this is a necessary
task, and someone has to do it, and since no one else is doing it,
that someone has to be you.

Apart from this, it's useful to say what the special function is *not*. It is not necessarily something overtly "spiritual." A man may have a special function as a housing contractor. After all, the world needs houses, and to be an honest and capable contractor is not a small thing. The accountant who decides to chuck it all and become a massage therapist has not necessarily found her special function. She may be running away from her true responsibilities in a field where consciousness and integrity are very much needed. In certain cases, an individual may even have to serve as the single spark of light and goodness in a corrupt organization. Obviously this situation carries the risk of being corrupted oneself, but at times it may be necessary.

I admit that it's not always so simple. We live in a highly specialized society, where jobs often involve performing some small function in a much larger network. Say you work at the phone company, and your job is to change people's phone numbers. This is obviously a valuable service, but you can easily ask if this is what you came to this earth to do. Some people get a lot of satisfaction out of doing routine jobs and look outside the workplace—to their families, their communities, their churches—to give a broader meaning to their lives. Others may never wonder what their life purpose is at all; they are too busy simply making ends meet. Still others know all too well what they are supposed to do but run away from it, like the prophets Jeremiah and Jonah in the Bible. In any case, your special function is something that only you can discover.

Finally, there are the very limited and transient special functions. A couple of examples will best explain what I mean. It was New Year's night (that is, the day after New Year's Eve), probably 2002 or 2003, and I was in New York. I had stayed out very late drinking with an old friend, and came back to the apartment where I was staying around three thirty or four in the morning. I could not get the key to work in the lock. I was using the right key, but I simply couldn't get it to turn. I was the only person staying there, so there was no one to let me in.

I decided to go down to an all-night store on the corner and buy some graphite to lubricate the lock. (I didn't know whether a convenience store would carry such a thing, but I desperately hoped it would.) On my way there, I found some people standing around a man who was lying on the sidewalk. He had been hit by some thugs; I gathered it was a gay-bashing incident (this was in the East Village). Someone had already called 911, but for some reason I felt the need to stay there until the ambulance arrived. I did very little except to tell the man to stay calm and awake, reassure him that help was coming, and calm a young woman who was starting to panic. After the ambulance came, I went to the store, bought the graphite, and was able to open the lock. I have no idea what happened to the man afterward.

There was nothing out of the ordinary about this. The lock had been sticking all along, and I'd had trouble with it before. I did nothing for the victim that any number of people couldn't have done, and in any case there were others around to help. Still, for some reason it was necessary for me to be there for those few minutes. That was my special function at that time and place. I imagine most people have had experiences of this kind.

To take a better-known example, in August 2013 there was a road accident in Missouri. A vehicle flipped, trapping a young woman inside. Rescue workers could not get her out, and her vital signs began to fail. At that point a mysterious priest showed up, anointed and prayed with her, and spoke to her reassuringly. Her vital signs improved, and finally other rescue workers came who could turn over the car. No one locally was able to identify the priest, and none of the sixty-nine photographs taken of the incident showed him. The story captured the public imagination, and some said he must have been an angel.

In the end he came forward and turned out to be a flesh-and-blood priest named Patrick Dowling. Evidently Dowling's special function at that time was to be present at that accident and give a blessing where it was needed.

I have trouble forgiving my situation. I can forgive people,
but I'm going through some hard times and I find it hard
to forgive this.

It can be a problem. Say you are going through some serious medical or financial difficulties. You may be angry or fearful, and these feelings can be hard to shake. Sometimes people have no one to blame but themselves, but there are just as many cases where they are clearly no one's fault.

Let's take a quick look at some of the main explanations given for life difficulties: (1) They are tests and trials that God is putting you through in order to teach you a lesson or make you a better person; (2) they are the result of impersonal forces, such as karma or the influence of the planets; (3) they are simply the result of chance, and this time around you happen to be the unlucky one.

These can be broken down into two main possibilities: either the things that you are going through are meaningless and random or they are meaningful. In either case, the outcome is the same. You have to deal with the situation whether it is meaningful or meaningless.

Most people, however, are happier when they see a purpose to their lives, particularly in times of struggle, and it may be part of our task as humans to create meaning when there is none. Certainly many people are made wiser and more compassionate by their troubles. A friend of mine who has been unemployed for two years sent me an e-mail that said, "Having encountered my own dark night of the soul has made me more empathetic to the troubles of my closest friends." On the other hand, those who have never known major misfortune can often seem callous. As the Roman emperor and philosopher Marcus Aurelius wrote, "As a general rule, those amongst us who rank as patricians are somewhat wanting in natural affection."

It's true that after a certain point this is not much consolation, and we find ourselves wondering if there isn't a better way to make us into good people.

Maybe a story will help us understand our situation more clearly.

A long time ago, a man and a woman who lived in a state of complete happiness came to God and said, "We've heard that there's this thing called good and evil, and we'd like to know what it is." God replied, "That is not a good idea. I do not advise you to do this." But they said, "Come on, we want to." And God said, "Very well. But you are going to have to live in a world where it hurts to have babies and you have to work hard for a living." And the man and woman were sent down to earth.

You can see that this is nothing more than a retelling of the

story of the Fall from Genesis. In this light it is a profound statement about the human condition. "In sorrow thou shalt bring
forth children . . . In the sweat of thy face shall thou eat bread,
till thou return to the ground" (Genesis 3:16, 19). We do have to
work hard for a living, and it hurts very much to have babies. We
have chosen to know good and evil, and the only way to know
these things is to experience them.

Of course I'm a complete stranger to you who are reading this
book. But I'm willing to make the following statement with abso-
lute certainty: You have known both good and evil. Everyone has.
It's true that the proportions seem to vary widely from person to
person, and ultimately no one really knows why. Maybe it's karma
or astrological aspects or God testing us, or some combination of
these. (I myself believe that both karma and astrological influences
play powerful roles in our destinies; the will of God is a bit more
inscrutable.) But every human being on this planet, no matter how
wretched or exalted, has known some good and evil in life. It is our
condition, and it may have something to do with our reason for
being here.

Can you imagine things that you couldn't forgive?

Easily. I've known hardships in life. I've lost jobs, had marriages fail, been hard up for money. These things were all difficult for me to bear. At the same time I realize that they are nothing compared to what some people have to go through.

Offhand I can think of half a dozen things that could happen to me that I would have to struggle mightily to forgive. And these are all personal things—having to do with health, death, money, and so on. But what if I witnessed some enormous crime against humanity?

My father was a sailor in China in the 1930s, in that long-gone era when the United States had gunboats sailing up and down the Yangtze to protect American missionaries and commercial interests. During that time, in 1937–38, the Japanese army carried out the Rape of Nanking, in which masses of Chinese, possibly as many as three hundred thousand, were massacred over a six-week period. Soldiers lined up civilians on the street and hacked them to bits for sword practice. Author Simon Winchester writes, "Contests were held to see how many heads could be cut off with a single sword blade—the winner claimed 106, and his victory made headlines in the Tokyo press." My father was there for at least part of it. I can't say what he did or didn't see. All he would say was that he thought he would never sleep again.

Like most men of what is now called the Greatest Generation, my father was not given to talking about such matters. As a result I don't know how he came to terms with this experience personally (as well as everything else he must have witnessed during twenty years of military service that included the Second World War). But he didn't seem to like the Japanese very much.

What would I personally feel or do if I witnessed something on that scale? Of course we all think we know how we would respond. We would be merciful, compassionate, consummately helpful. We would forgive. Or, taking the other tack, we might imagine ourselves as vindicators, agents of righteous judgment. But imaginings and reality are two very different things.

Joseph Conrad's novel *Lord Jim* is about this dilemma. Jim, an English sailor, has visions of himself as a great hero. But at one point he is part of the crew of a rundown ship that is taking Muslim pilgrims to Mecca. Something goes wrong with the ship, and the crew decides that it is going to sink. So, in the middle of the night, while all the pilgrims are asleep, they let down the lifeboats and desert the ship—the ultimate act of cowardice for sailors. Jim is the last to go. For a moment he lingers on the ship's edge, his heroism and his instinct for self-preservation at war within him.

Finally he jumps. In fact, the ship does not sink; it is rescued by another ship that is passing by a day or so later. The rest of the novel describes how Jim comes to terms with his moment of moral failure.

Unless I've been in a situation like that myself, I don't know how I would act. People do surprising things. Someone you thought was vile turns out to be a hero; someone you looked up to proves to be a disappointment. You have no way of knowing in advance which kind of person you are.

So I don't know what I might or might not be able to forgive. But look at where this train of thought will lead. No matter how many misfortunes you have suffered, no matter how much hardship you have gone through, you can always imagine something worse—and of course there always is something worse.

I'm reminded of a joke I heard while I was living in Tennessee. During the New Deal, the government decided to take stock of poverty in Appalachia. So a government worker went around to talk to people in the hills. He came across an old woman in a torn and patched dress, living in a falling-down shack. He talked a little with the woman about her situation. Then he asked her, "What would you do if you had an extra five hundred dollars a year?" The woman thought a moment and said, "Reckon I'd give it to the poor."

No matter how hard your lot, there is always someone worse off, and there is always some way your own situation can be harder. The mind is a great artist and can construct the most horrible as well as the most beautiful possibilities. If you use it to write scenarios of future disasters, you will find yourself beset with fear and anxiety. Probably the best approach is to forgive as well as you can for now, and leave the future to the future. As Christ says in the Sermon on the Mount, "Sufficient unto the day is the evil thereof" (Matthew 6:34).

Can forgiveness make me successful?

People generally think of success in terms of four things: love, money, status, and power. The order of importance of these varies a great deal from person to person, as does the amount of value placed on each.

As you've probably discovered, this is not another book in the "think and grow rich" category, nor does it talk about using mental power to make your dreams come true. (I'll say a little bit more about this in the next chapter.)

I don't think forgiveness will lead to material success. Material success is elusive and comes from a combination of luck, talent, and hard work—usually large quantities of all three. Forgiveness in and of itself will not provide you with these.

Nevertheless, forgiveness can help, at least indirectly. The things you let go of when you forgive—grudges, resentments, grievances, and so on—often serve as impediments to success whether you realize it or not.

Say you want to find a lover. The Deal will not make you more physically attractive. But it can make you more *personally* attractive. That's simply because people with grudges are often unpleasant to be around, so if you have a lot of grudges, someone is unlikely to want to spend time with you. If you have a light, forgiving, carefree attitude, someone is more likely to want to be with you.

The same is true with wealth, power, and fame. If you are a gloomy, resentful person, it's much harder to get people to buy your product or elect you to high office or give you the lead in their next film.

In short, grievances are an encumbrance that can keep you from attaining your life's goals. Removing them will not, I suspect, in and of itself lead to success. But it will take away some of the major barriers.

There is, of course, another side to this, because there are those in life who succeed by appealing to people's fear and greed and hatred. Each of us possesses enough of these qualities that we can easily be manipulated, as I've already said. (Much of marketing today works by playing to, or creating, a sense of fear or inadequacy.) If you are sufficiently calculating and cynical, you can make use of these weaknesses to get ahead, to make lots of money and amass a great deal of power. Others use their grievances as clubs with which to bludgeon others and make them submit.

What are the drawbacks to doing this? You know the usual answers: bad karma, the wrath of God, and so on. But let me mention another. If you take that route, you become a manipulator, a bully, a cheat. There is no getting out of this fate; as philosophers sometimes say, you are what you do. You become your own punishment.

What does forgiveness have to do with love and compassion?

These three things are related but not identical. Here is how I see them.

I would define love as that which unites self and other, while preserving the integrity of each. By the latter phrase I mean this: you could say that the lion loves the lamb. The lion loves the lamb so much that it wants to make it part of itself. But we don't think of this as love. Love, as we usually understand it, wants to unite with the other, but also to preserve and enjoy the other *as* other.

Love comes in many forms, and usually has some strings attached (I talk about this in my book *Conscious Love*). You may love your friend, but if he doesn't return your phone calls or texts and never has time to see you, eventually you get the message and let him drop. You may fall in love with someone, but she may not reciprocate, and at some point you have to let the whole thing go. Unconditional love does exist. It's just rarer than it's generally imagined to be.

If you love someone, you don't have to feel sorry for her. You may, for one reason or another, but it's not essential to what love is. With compassion, it's different. With compassion, there is almost always some element of feeling sorry, whether this is mildly or strongly felt. Love may or may not be in the picture. You can feel compassion for victims of a catastrophic flood or hurricane without necessarily loving them.

Buddhism stresses compassion; it talks much less about love than Christianity does. This is not an accident. To feel compassion for someone, you have to believe he is suffering to some degree. For Buddhists, this comes naturally, because, according to Buddhist teaching, all beings are suffering. Even though a creature may not actually be in pain at a given moment, it is still suffering from conditioned existence—meaning a sense of separation from the One Mind that encompasses all.

Whether or not you accept this view of things, Buddhism has a beautiful teaching about love and compassion. The teaching is called "the four immeasurable qualities of being." These are love, compassion, joy, and equanimity. They balance one another out.

Say you feel love for someone. If you take this beyond a certain point, you can grow attached to her in a possessive and unhealthy way. You counteract this with a feeling of compassion, remembering that she too is a human being, who knows suffering just as we all do. But compassion can also be taken to extremes. You can become very morose dwelling on all the suffering in the world. You counteract this by acknowledging and feeling the joy in the universe. Taken too far, however, joy becomes a kind of delusory euphoria. You counteract this with equanimity. But if you dwell too much on equanimity, you can become dull and apathetic. You counteract this with love, bringing us back to the beginning of the cycle.

The cycle, then, looks like this, and of course it can start anywhere:

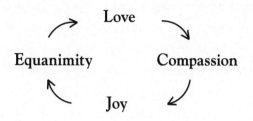

Forgiveness, you'll notice, is not part of the cycle. And it's not quite the same as either love or compassion. You can forgive someone without loving or feeling compassion for him. The essential thing that defines forgiveness is that it involves a belief that the person who is being forgiven has done something wrong.

If someone says, "I'm sorry," and you say, "There's nothing to be sorry about," you're saying that there's no need for forgiveness because no harm has been done. But if you feel the need for forgiveness—whether toward yourself or someone else—there is almost always a problem in the background, whether it's a moral failing or a simple mistake.

This sense of a problem lurking somewhere in the background is almost always present. You may even notice that in your mind, no sooner is one problem solved than another rises up to take its place. In fact you could say that man is the animal that believes something is wrong.

This "something wrong" plays a very peculiar role in our lives. We seem to differ from the other animals at least in this respect: Say your cat is comfortable and well fed. If so, then generally it seems perfectly content. With humans, it is not so. We can have all our needs met—for food and love and status and so on—and still have this irritating background sense that something is wrong. Certain twentieth-century philosophers gave this condition the grandiose name of "existential angst."

Many words have been written and uttered trying to get to the root of this sense of "something wrong." Sometimes it is presented as a cognitive error—an error in the way we're thinking. The Greek philosopher Socrates said that all evil was due to ignorance, and the Buddhists say that suffering arises from a primordial forgetting of our true, enlightened nature.

Usually, however, the problem is stated in moral terms. The Fall from Genesis, as conventionally understood, is a rebellion by the primal human pair against the will of God. While Christianity has often been criticized for positing this "original sin" at the beginning of everything, it is found in a remarkably wide range of places.

Recently I read a book called *The Origins of the World's Mythologies* by a Harvard professor named E. J. Michael Witzel. Comparing mythologies all over the world, he found some themes that were almost universal—from Australian aborigines to Native Americans to the Greeks and Romans to the Christian West. Some, he says, even go back to the time when the whole human species still lived in Africa.

One of these themes, curiously, is the story of a flood that destroyed almost all of humankind. We know it through the Genesis story of Noah, but it is found almost everywhere. A theme that usually accompanies it is the idea that this flood came about because the gods were offended by the sin of humans— usually some form of pride—and decided to punish them.

So there is a universal theme of human separation from the divine, and moreover of a colossal act of sin that was the cause. Why this story is so widespread is too big a question to go into here, and anyway it is not relevant. The point is that this sense of something wrong seems to pervade the human mind worldwide.

Without going too deep into this issue, I would say that one major component of this sense of "something wrong" is what I have called grievances. The human mind, for reasons that we may not fully understand, often acts as if it's conditioned to think in terms of grievances, sin, punishment, and guilt. While it's true that bad things do happen and there is such a thing as personal responsibility, this mechanism of guilt has taken over to the point where we see everything through its lens.

Which is why this book offers a program of total forgiveness. It is a way of disarming this mechanism in the mind and freeing us from useless grievances and guilt. In this way it may help uproot the underlying sense of something wrong that sours our lives.

I have this strange fear. I'm afraid that if I forgive completely, life, or God, will somehow compensate by throwing bigger and bigger things at me to forgive.

It's sometimes said that there are only two basic emotions: love and fear. It has also been said that perfect love casteth out fear. But we rarely attain perfect love, and fears seem to be ever present in our lives.

In regard to fear, I would say something similar to what I said about grievances. At some deep level, we think that our fear protects us—that if we didn't go around terrified at the prospect of every possible disaster, we would have our bones picked clean in a few minutes.

But fear is, for the most part, dysfunctional. Fear doesn't protect us; it incapacitates us. Even in extreme situations it may not be as useful as you think. If a bear started chasing you, probably the first thing you would do is run—even before you felt any emotional fear at all.

All the same, this emotion runs very deep. It sometimes feels as if the human mind is sitting on a kind of water table of fear that lies beneath the surface of consciousness, gushing up often— or usually—at the most unexpected times. To tap into this and release it completely is a big task, and I doubt that there are many who have succeeded.

Fears and grievances aren't, of course, the same thing. But they do seem to be closely intertwined. Releasing grievances can help release fear. Why? Because if you forgive, you're less likely to see your fellow humans as a collection of villains and enemies who are out to get you. You're more likely to see them as ordinary people like yourself, who are trying to get through life and achieve some measure of happiness, sometimes succeeding, sometimes failing—even ludicrously.

It has occurred to me that you can't achieve spiritual awakening above a certain level unless you're able to see yourself as a comic character in a world full of comic characters. Certainly we all look that way sometimes—and people who look comic usually aren't very frightening.

I'm troubled by the idea that you can make a deal with God.

People often make deals with God. My father, for example, never drank alcohol in all the time I knew him. (Only once, with great reluctance, did he eat some brandied peaches that someone had given us at Christmas.) For some reason—probably because I suspected I wouldn't get much of an answer—I never asked him why, although I did once ask my mother. She said, rather vaguely, "It was because of a promise he made in the war." I gathered that my father had, in some moment of danger in wartime, promised God that he would give up alcohol for good if he got out of this scrape.

Years later, when I was working for a farm magazine in California (which is a long story in itself), I noticed that one of our field editors didn't drink, and I asked him why. He said that his daughter had been born with a birth defect—or at any rate they thought she had—and he had made a similar vow: if his daughter turned out to be normal and healthy, he would give up alcohol for good. Evidently she did turn out to be all right.

Even though, as these examples suggest, people often feel that God comes through with his side of the bargain, there does seem to be something odd about deals of this kind. Why wouldn't God answer a prayer even without some kind of tempting offer dangled in front of his nose? Furthermore, an almighty and infinite Being is not going to need anything from us.

As I suggested in my book *Conscious Love*, much of what we call love is in fact transactional and highly conditional. We attach many strings to our behavior, and it's hard to imagine a human society that didn't work this way, at least to some degree. So it's natural that we would view our relations with God in the same fashion.

Is the Deal, then, a bargain with God? In some ways, I suppose it is. But on the other hand, we are called upon to forgive in any case—to have our debts forgiven as we have forgiven our debtors.

Besides, as the examples above suggest, deals with God often seem to work.

You made a big point about the fact that the line in the Lord's Prayer says, "Forgive us our debts." Does that apply to financial debts too?

Well, you can certainly call your lenders and try to explain the Deal to them, but I suspect that it would be a waste of time.

That much said, there can be value in forgiving debts in the literal sense. Someone has borrowed a hundred dollars from you, and, to look at it realistically, you are never going to get this money back. This happens to everyone: practically all of us have had some debts that we could not and did not repay—or that someone else repaid for us. From the point of view of the Deal, it might be a good idea to bear this in mind and simply let the debt go—either by telling the other person that he doesn't have to pay you back, or simply making no more mention of it.

Forgiving debts may not sound like good financial policy on a larger level, but maybe it is. You may remember the biblical practice of the jubilee, whereby all debts were cleared at the end of a certain number of years. At the end of his highly praised book *Debt: The First 5,000 Years*, David Graeber writes:

> It seems to me that we are long overdue for some kind of Biblical-style Jubilee: one that would affect both international debt and consumer debt. It would be salutary not just because it would relieve so much genuine human suffering, but also because it would be our way of reminding ourselves that money is not ineffable, that paying one's debts is not the essence of morality, that all these things are human arrangements and that if democracy is to mean anything, it is the ability to all agree to arrange things in a different way.

I personally am not going to stand around and wait for this jubilee to come about, but I still think forgiveness of debts can be a valuable and instructive practice for individuals.

You may or may not see some (positive) karmic consequences from your actions, but in any case it's usually wise not to look for any specific results from what you are doing. Results will no doubt come, but in a different form and from a different direction from the one you had expected.

While we're on the subject of karma, you make it sound like this: If I forgive fully, all my bad karma will be cleared. After that, I will be immune to any misfortune in the future. Right?

If I were to promise that, as a result of doing the Deal or anything else, you will never suffer misfortune again, I would be insane and you would be right to disbelieve everything I said. No one can make this promise. (Perhaps God can, but he never does.)

Moreover, the concept of karma is problematic: it says that evil deeds will beget evil and good deeds will beget good. But it also has to account for the fact that this compensation doesn't always occur right away, or, apparently in some cases, ever. This may be why religions that teach karma also teach reincarnation, which is a way of explaining apparent injustices in the world. If you suffer needlessly, it's because you sinned in a previous life. If you do wrong and are never caught or punished, you will pay for it in a later life.

The theories that try to account for these long-term delays in retribution are intricate and not always convincing. Sometimes karmic influences are described as a kind of seed that will lie dormant until it finds the right conditions to flourish in. But then it seems that these seeds can take lifetimes to flourish, and the reincarnated person who suffers for her sins in a previous life will have absolutely no memory of these sins or any concept of why she is suffering now.

As I said, the idea of karma is problematic. After all, even if the state were to pull a murderer off the street and execute him without the slightest explanation, the murderer would still probably have an inkling of why this was happening to him. The victim of karma has none.

That's why you'll notice that I have always discussed karma in this book as a possibility rather than a certainty. An old spiritual maxim that I was taught early on is "Neither accept nor reject." If you apply this principle to many such things as karma, you will spare yourself a great deal of anxiety and may even open yourself to some unexpected insights.

Nevertheless, to repeat a point that I made earlier, there does seem to be some truth in the law of karma, and most people understand this intuitively, even if its operations are mysterious and inexplicable at times. If you forgive, you will, I'm convinced, receive forgiveness yourself.

Is there any age limit that you would recommend for the Deal?

You should be old enough to be able to read—or at least understand—the instructions. Apart from that, there is no limit. I suspect that if a child did the Deal, something very beautiful and powerful would come out of it. But it would be a serious mistake for a parent to pressure a child into doing the Deal.

Do you have any suggestions for applying forgiveness to social media and things I see on the Internet?

Social media have arisen so fast that we're still not quite sure about their consequences. But we can say two things.

In the first place, the whole complex of new communications technology—e-mail, social media, the smartphone, and so on—make responses almost instantaneous. A bored fifteen-year-old can text "This class sux" to his friend and it will be received right away.

Furthermore, these devices make it possible to respond in complete isolation from the people you're responding to. If you say something nasty in person or even on the phone, you may have to deal with consequences. If you post a hostile message on Facebook, not only will you not face any immediate consequences, but the person you insult may be on a different continent.

As a result, social media have weakened our impulse control. You can easily send messages that you would never have the guts to utter in person.

Unfortunately, impulse control is one of the features that make human society possible. If everyone were to start screaming or hitting the minute they felt like it, there would be no such thing as civilized existence.

In the first place, then, it's probably wise to learn (or relearn) the habit of impulse control while you are on the Internet. Usually it seems to be a good idea to wait at least overnight before you write or send anything genuinely nasty—simply as a matter of common-sense prudence. It's a way of fulfilling what I think of as the eleventh commandment: "Do not make unnecessary enemies."

In the second place, taking forgiveness seriously as a long-term practice will definitely change your impulses. Forgiveness, like everything else, is a matter of habit and conditioning. The more you accustom yourself to practicing it, the easier and more natural it becomes. At some point in the not-too-distant future, negative impulses will be weaker and will surface less often.

Do I need to ask for forgiveness from others?

This falls into the category of external actions about which you will have to decide for yourself. Sometimes it's inappropriate to ask explicitly for forgiveness. Calling someone up from thirty years in the past may be annoying and counterproductive. But the choice is yours and yours alone.

The same holds true for offering forgiveness. Often it is best not to do so explicitly, since, as we've seen, this is a message that could well be misunderstood. You may find it better to express your new attitude more subtly, simply by being kinder.

One important point: you cannot and should not expect any changes in anyone else's external behavior as a result of your forgiveness. Changes may occur, or they may not. *You have no control over others' reactions.* You will be wiser and happier if you take this truth to heart.

Sometimes you sound as if you don't want to commit yourself in matters of religion.

That's deliberate. I've written several previous books that describe my views on these matters—especially *Inner Christianity,*

Conscious Love, and *The Dice Game of Shiva*. If you're interested in what I think about religion in more detail, please read them.

But this book is about forgiveness, and I have tried to make it as accessible as I can. I've stressed that the Deal is open to people of all faiths and of none. It doesn't serve my purpose to make a stand on theological issues here.

By whose authority are you telling us all this?

As a matter of fact, I haven't dwelled very much on my background or credentials. This too is deliberate.

In the end, there is only one authority: you. Even if you choose to evaluate someone on the basis of credentials and certificates, it is still you in the end who bestows the authority. If you accept the authority of a church or hierarchy, this is still the case.

Thus you can really evaluate this material only by one criterion: whether it makes sense to you and resonates with you. If it doesn't, no quantity of credentials will make much difference—nor should it. If it does, then you have something you can work with.

6

THE
WISH-FULFILLING
JEWEL

The lore and legends of the world sometimes speak of a secret that will solve all your problems and fulfill all your dreams. Some would say that this key has to do with thought power: all you have to do is harness the power of your mind to make your wishes come true.

Is there any truth to this idea? If so, why don't we all have what we want? If not, why has this idea hung on for so long?

To some degree, this belief can be chalked up to wishful thinking (which in itself attests to the power of thought). But not all of it.

The mind does possess tremendous power. We're often told that we use only a tiny amount of its capacity. But no one explains why.

If you look into your own mind, you will find all kinds of things going on: plans, memories, grudges, resentments, fantasies, daydreams, illusions. Many of these impulses conflict with one another. You dislike someone but feel guilty about it. You are attracted to someone else but are afraid to show it.

In short, if there were such a thing as thought power, it would produce a world of conflicts, tensions, ambiguities, unexpected successes, and astonishing failures. Which, when you look at it, is the world we live in.

Indeed, there is some evidence that thoughts have power in shaping our reality. It's probably true that if you can control your thoughts, you can control your reality—certainly to a much greater extent than most of us do.

There's one small problem, though. The Buddha once said that it is easier to go into battle single-handed against a thousand enemies, each of them armed to the teeth, and conquer them a thousand times than it is to conquer the mind. So to say that all you have to do is control the mind is like saying that you could have all the power you need if you could only harness the Atlantic Ocean.

The Dweller on the Threshold

Still, it seems to be true that if you focus your thoughts on a certain goal and feed them with some emotional energy, you stand a greater chance for success.

In fact, I'm convinced that at a certain level of the mind, to think of something is to make it happen—literally and in the physical world. But this part of the mind is very heavily barricaded (since it would be dangerous to have access to it for anyone who is not highly trained, and probably even then). This mental barricade is not known in conventional psychology, but some mystical literature calls it the Guardian on the Threshold or the Dweller on the Threshold. It is not the Devil—if by the Devil you mean the metaphysical power of evil in the universe—but if you see it, it will look like the Devil to you. That's its job: to scare you off.

Normally people don't end up having to face the Dweller on the Threshold; as I say, this is in a deeply guarded layer of the mind. Certain spiritual practices, and certain drugs, can give access to it, and can even disable it to some degree. That's partly why there are so many warnings about these practices. (If you want to learn more about the Dweller on the Threshold, you can read a somewhat sensationalized account of it in *Zanoni* by the nineteenth-century English novelist Edward Bulwer-Lytton.)

But to go back to thought power in its better-known form, we can ask whether the Deal will help us master this power. The answer is clear: to the extent that you have managed to clear your mind of unnecessary guilt and grievances, which sap its power, you will have that much more energy to harness toward your goals—whether we are talking about using thought power in some metaphysical sense or in the sense of simply having more time and energy to devote to them.

But as I have already said, the Deal in and of itself will not necessarily make you more successful in terms of romance, money, or power.

Entering the Mystery

There is, however, another secret. This secret is much more important and profound than simply saying you can harness the power of the mind to get what you want. It's sometimes called the Wish-Fulfilling Jewel.

It has many other names as well. We will get to them a little later. But the best way to investigate it is by means of another exercise. You will recognize this because it's similar to the beginning of the exercise you did with the Deal.

1. Sense the Body.

Sit upright in a chair, or in a cross-legged position, or take any position in which you feel comfortable but alert.

Begin by closing your eyes and sensing your body in your seat. You may be aware of your back against the chair, your feet on the floor, your hands on your thighs or wherever they happen to be. See if you can consciously sense them from the inside. If the mind settles, you can feel the sensations rise and fall, in different parts of the body at different moments. You may feel them as waves or ripples of energy.

As you do, you will possibly notice something very curious about these sensations. You may feel a slight distance from them. They may feel less like me or mine than waves in an ocean or a stream—things that come and go in their own time.

Now let your attention come to the breath. You can take a couple of deep breaths to relax, but otherwise don't try to control or

manipulate the flow. Just let it go in and out and watch its progress as if you were sitting by a pleasant brook and watching the
water go by. Do this for a couple of minutes.

2. Watch the Thoughts.

All this time, thoughts and images and pictures are arising in
your mind. Simply sit back and watch the images in your mind's
eye as if you were watching a film. Their content does not matter
one way or another. What is important is that you watch these
things in your mind clearly and impartially, almost as if they
belonged to somebody else. Usually you think these thoughts and
images are you. But if you can step back and watch them from a
distance, you must be something other than these things.

Emotions—anxiety, anger, or, for that matter, cheer or joy—
may come up along with the thoughts and images; an image may
trigger an emotion, or emotions that you feel may bring up images
in the mind. Thoughts and emotions are tightly connected, so
simply watch them all together as they arise in their turn.

3. Focus on the Watcher.

Let your attention now rest on the part of yourself that is doing the watching. It can't be your body, because you can experience the body as if it belonged to someone else. It can't be your
thoughts, because you can look at these too from a distance, like
a spectator watching a film. You will never see this watcher in
yourself, because it is always the part that is doing the seeing, but
you can become aware of its presence if you try.

Saint Francis of Assisi once said, "What you are looking for is
what is looking."

Let your attention rest in this silent watcher. Sensations,
thoughts, and images will continue to come up, but continue to
watch them as if they were a film on a screen. All of these things
that you thought were yourself are passing here before you. So
who are you?

What you really are is this silent watcher within. It experiences everything, but it is none of the things it experiences. This
is your true "I."

Now gradually let your attention return to its ordinary state.
Become aware of your sensations, the breath, the feeling of your

body in the chair. When it's comfortable, you can open your eyes and come back to where you are now.

The God Within

The truth is that, underneath all of the pain and pleasure and worries and grievances, there is something in you that says "I."

I once said this during a talk I was giving to a roomful of people disabled with multiple sclerosis. When I did, most of them nodded, even the ones who could barely move.

Here are some other names that have been given to this part of yourself: the witness, the silent watcher, the true Self, "I am." Each of these illustrates some aspect of this watcher. It has also been called "the God within." That is, it is the place within you where you connect with God.

Deep down inside, you know these things. The exercise here was simply a reminder, a way to bring them to the foreground of your consciousness.

If you have some understanding—that is, understanding through experience—of these truths, you will find that much of the spiritual literature of the world becomes clearer and less mysterious. In the Gospels, for example, Christ keeps talking about an entity called "the kingdom of heaven" or "the kingdom of God." It is this Self that he is talking about.

This entity is very small, like a mustard seed, but it gives birth to the whole tree of your experience. It is like a treasure buried deep in the field of your mind. It is like a little bit of leaven, which leavens the whole lump. It is like a coin that a woman lost.

Christ speaks this way in the synoptic Gospels: Matthew, Mark, and Luke. He refers to the kingdom of heaven and speaks in parables. In the Gospel of John he does not do this. He does not speak in parables. He speaks in "I am" statements: "I am the way, the truth, and the life." "I am the door." "I and the Father are one." This is not necessarily Jesus the man speaking about himself personally. He is telling us something about this "I" within.

I've digressed here to speak a little bit about Christianity, because Christianity is the dominant religion in our culture, and we see these terms and phrases very frequently without having any idea of what they mean. I could have used the language of Judaism, Hinduism, Buddhism, Islam, or any number of other faiths. I haven't done so simply because they are less familiar to most people in our society.

You may be asking what all this has to do with the Deal or with forgiveness. It is this: In most of us most of the time, this "I" is lost or forgotten because it has identified itself with its experience. It has thoughts and emotions and believes it *is* those things. Grievances are among the strongest of these entanglements. If you let go of them, you will have a stronger connection with this "I" that is your true Self.

Conversely, the realization that you are this "I," and not what the "I" experiences, will make it easier to let go of your grievances. You will understand that they are not you, but annoying encumbrances that you have mistaken for you.

If you have some real glimpse of this "I" in you, you can still go ahead and use your thought power to find your dream job or dream lover. But all in all you will probably be more motivated to look within and see into the deeper reaches of the "I."

7

THE UPPER ROOM

GROUP WORK

By this point, at the very least, you realize that you're not your sports team.

You also realize that you are not your grievances.

This is more than many people grasp in their entire lifetimes. This knowledge can't be called enlightenment, perhaps, but it's still a major awakening. And it can be hard to share your awakening with someone else, since words very often don't do it justice.

This can lead to a sense of isolation, and in this isolation it may be difficult to keep a sense of the Deal alive.

There is, after all, very little to reinforce it in everyday life. While there is a vague cultural ideal that forgiveness is a good thing, it's not actively promoted, except maybe for a few days around Christmas. Quite the opposite—resentments, hostilities, hatreds, suspicions—are the things that are reinforced in our culture. We see the consequences all around us. People sometimes look at the world and wonder how it could be the way it is, but it would make more sense to ask how the world could be otherwise.

Having done the Deal, one becomes less concerned with upsets large and small. After all, total forgiveness encompasses even the saddest and most broken aspects of the world. And it has to include even the grievances and grudges that you may—and will—still hear about from others.

Nevertheless, that does not get around the problem of isolation.

For this reason, although the Deal is a completely individual process and can be done by anyone anytime, there might be some wisdom in some kind of group reinforcement. Either a number of people get together and do the Deal, or having done it on their own, they meet on a regular basis and support one another.

Group Structure

This can be done in any number of ways. In my experience, it's best to have a modicum of structure so that the group keeps to its purpose. Certainly it's best to eliminate disturbances as much as possible: avoid having people (including children) running in and out, and shut off phones (however difficult this may be for some). The group will also probably work better if there is a single facilitator—one person who officially starts and closes the group and who can give some direction and focus where it's needed. This need not be the same person every time, although, if the meeting is at a private home, it usually works best if the moderator is also the host.

A formal beginning and ending are recommended. These can be as intricate or as simple as you like—most people today tend to favor simplicity, and ritual for its own sake can become an obstacle. One approach is to start and end with a short nonsectarian prayer, possibly accompanied by some simple act like lighting a candle. This makes it easier to create a sacred space in which to work.

We don't need to get terribly mystical or superstitious about the idea of a sacred space. Essentially it's nothing more than a particular time and place where several people have gathered for a purpose that is higher than mundane concerns and have agreed to focus on that purpose for a while. In the case of a group that's based on the Deal, this purpose would have to do with forgiveness and applying it in daily life.

Often, when a group meets in this way for some time, it begins to develop its own atmosphere and quality. The quality of the space changes; there is a greater sense of stillness and presence, even when people are talking. There even may be a sense of being above the usual run of ordinary life. That is why in some mystical literature this is called an "upper room." It has nothing to do with the story of the building that it's on; it has to do with a sense of elevation and, perhaps, seclusion from the rest of the world, even if this lasts for only an hour.

The facilitator has two chief functions: to make sure that the group stays focused on its purpose and to encourage people to participate more or less equally. This doesn't always mean that everyone has to speak for the same amount of time. It does mean that everyone present should speak at least a little and that no one monopolizes the time. Usually in a group of any size, there are one or two people who love to do all the talking, and if they are not (gently) reined in, they will take over and make the group their own personal platform, and the group will soon fall apart. People can be quite funny about this. There is a type of person who starts out shyly, saying something like, "It's hard for me to talk in a group like this," and then proceeds to babble on for fifteen minutes.

Others, of course, barely talk at all, and while it's not always a bad thing to be a quiet person, there's a big difference between a quiet person who is present and paying attention and a quiet person who is literally or figuratively asleep. Both types can usually be recognized easily enough.

One way of dealing with this issue is the old technique of the "talking stick." This object—it can be a stick, a stone, a crystal, or, for that matter, a bottle cap—is placed in the center of the group, on a coffee table, say, and each person picks it up before speaking. She then speaks for as long as she feels it's appropriate, then puts the object down, and someone else picks it up before speaking. This requires a little bit of discipline, since people are accustomed to back-and-forth conversations with interruptions, but it can help the group keep on target.

The other key is to stay focused on the actual purpose. Most people in groups like this tend to come from similar backgrounds and have similar beliefs and interests, so it can easily happen that the discussion veers off into politics or something of the kind. There is nothing wrong with this in itself, but if the conversation turns into harangues about how awful the president or Congress is, the group has lost its focus—not because of the subject matter, but because of the *attitude* people are taking toward the subject matter. I have been in any number of groups that were oriented around forgiveness where this sort of thing happened. It's not a crime or a tragedy, of course, but it will lower the level of the group, and if it goes too far in this direction, the group will turn into an ordinary social gathering and will most likely break up eventually.

Another useful form of structure is to limit the meeting to a finite amount of time—probably an hour or an hour and a half. People's attention spans tend to deteriorate after that time, and there will be a noticeable loss of energy and interest. Limiting the length of meetings also makes it easier for people to plan around them.

The frequency of meetings certainly can vary. Weekly meetings are ideal, but if the group can't meet more often than biweekly or monthly, that can work as well. If they're less frequent than monthly, it will be hard to maintain any sense of unity or continuity.

And then there are online meetings, chat rooms, discussion groups, and so on. For the most part I've found these less satisfying than face-to-face contact, though no doubt many would disagree. And online communication enables people to meet even if they're separated by large distances, which is valuable especially for those who are geographically isolated.

In these situations the rules will necessarily be more flexible, although at the very least the group should set some basic standards of decency and courtesy and have some way of excluding participants who don't follow them. It's also good to have a moderator who can enforce the rules. I haven't spent much time with unmoderated online groups, but I've been horrified by the postings I've seen on them. A version of Gresham's law seems to apply here: bad discussions drive out good.

8

FURTHERMORE

It's commonplace in this genre of writing to say, "This book will change your life." I will not say that. Instead I will say that this book *has* changed your life—whether you read it devotedly or whether you toss it aside never to look at again. Because now you know that you have a choice that you may not have known about before—the choice between grievances and total forgiveness. You also have an idea of what the choice means and what it can do. You can't unlearn this truth, and even if you forget you have ever read this book, its seeds may take root and grow in unexpected ways.

At this point it's time to close. Let me do so with some brief reminders for keeping the Deal alive:

Let it go.

You can deal with the vast majority of problems and issues in this way. You often don't even need to say or think "I forgive you"; you simply let the matter drop from your mind and heart. If you follow this practice long enough, it will become a habit, and many things that used to infuriate you will pass by almost unnoticed.

Affirm forgiveness daily.

This can be as simple as saying "I ask forgiveness for myself" or "I accept forgiveness for myself," and "I forgive everyone" or "I ask forgiveness for everyone." Of course you can adapt the wording to your preferences.

Send out blessings.

I've made this suggestion more than once, but this time I'll use the language of *A Course in Miracles*: "There is one thought in particular that should be remembered throughout the day. It is a thought of pure joy; a thought of peace, a thought of limitless release, limitless because all things are freed within it." You have not lost, and cannot lose, the power to bless. You need only to remember it.

———

One last word: There will be days—and even weeks and months—when you feel you have lost the thread of the Deal, have given up on it, or pushed it so far into the back of your mind that it no longer means anything to you. There will be other times, possibly long periods, when you have forgotten that you have done the Deal at all.

This is to be expected. The Deal goes against the grain of practically all of what the world stands for, so naturally resistance to it, both internal and external, will arise. But having done the Deal once, you can never lose it entirely. It will come back to you—sometimes by an outside reminder, sometimes by internal pain so intense that you remember that there was once a time when you had chosen a better way.

Remembering and forgetting and remembering again—these are recurrent themes in human life, and they figure greatly in the spiritual search. Perhaps in some strange way this process is itself a way of unifying the manifold contents of the mind. In any case, no matter how long it's been or how far you think you've strayed, you can always come back. As a spiritual teacher once said, "The work begins now."

RECOMMENDED READING

At this point some readers may want to know about books that may help them on the path. Of course I would recommend *A Course in Miracles*, although I know full well that it's not to everyone's taste. A small book, edited by Mary Strong and first published in the 1940s, is titled *Letters from the Scattered Brother-hood*. It contains short inspirational pieces that are, I believe, written from a high level of consciousness. Other sacred texts such as the *Tao Te Ching* and the *Bhagavad Gita* have inspired others, though they say very little about forgiveness as such.

Some works of fiction can also prove inspirational. Most inspirational literature is, from my point of view, of low literary and spiritual quality, but there are some impressive exceptions. W. Somerset Maugham's novel *The Razor's Edge* comes to mind.

Its hero is an American named Larry Darrell who is stunned by what he witnesses during World War I and then embarks upon a spiritual quest. The novel isn't so much about Larry's quest as such but about the influence he has on a small group of people. It has its own magic about it.

There are very few books that discuss spiritual group work in any kind of useful and specific way. In fact, the only one I know of is by my friend the British Kabbalist Warren Kenton, who writes under the name Z'ev ben Shimon Halevi. It's called *School of the Soul* (early editions are called *School of Kabbalah*), and it's excellent. Although it has a very specific kind of group in mind—one that is rooted in the Kabbalistic tradition—many of its ideas can be applied to the situations I talked about in the previous chapter.

And, of course, there is some wisdom in leaving oneself open to inspiration in your choice of reading. You may hear of something in an offhand discussion, you may come across a title in a bookshop, or a friend may recommend a book or pass it on to you. I have known several people who say they have had books literally fall off shelves into their hands. This rule holds true as well for websites, film clips, podcasts, and other forms of new media.

ACKNOWLEDGMENTS

To thank people who have taught you about forgiveness is to some extent a backhanded compliment, since of course it implies that they left you with something to forgive. If so, then, like most people, I would find myself with a long list, just as I would find myself on similar lists by many others.

Leaving aside these ambiguous examples, I would certainly like to thank my dear wife, Nicole, whose love and support have helped me through so many emotional ups and downs, and my sons, Robert and William, who have added so many new dimensions to my life. I would also like to thank my late aunt, Martha Palapis, to whom this book is dedicated, and who gave me so much from the time I was born to the time she died.

Professionally, profound gratitude is due first of all to my agent,

Laurie Fox, for her superb guidance in bringing this book to the world, and to Mitch Horowitz, my editor at Tarcher/Penguin, who has offered so much support and encouragement for my writing over the years. I would also like to thank the careful eye of copyeditor Diane Aronson, who has erased more than one blemish from this work.

Richard Smoley
Winfield, Illinois
June 2014

ABOUT THE AUTHOR

One of today's most highly regarded writers on esoteric spirituality, **Richard Smoley** is a graduate of Harvard College and the University of Oxford. He was a longtime editor of the venerated spiritual journal *Gnosis*. Smoley's books include *Supernatural: Writings on an Unknown History*; *Inner Christianity: A Guide to the Esoteric Tradition*; *The Dice Game of Shiva: How Consciousness Creates the Universe*; *Conscious Love: Insights from Mystical Christianity*; *The Essential Nostradamus*; *Forbidden Faith: The Secret History of Gnosticism*; and *Hidden Wisdom: A Guide to the Western Inner Traditions* (with Jay Kinney). Currently he is editor of *Quest: Journal of the Theosophical Society in America* and of Quest Books. He is online at www.richardsmoley.com.